Big-Bass Secrets

CATCH TROPHY LARGEMOUTHS AND SMALLMOUTHS WITH THE EXPERTS OF Outdoor Life

CREATIVE PUBLISHING international

MINNETONKA, MINNESOTA

Creative Publishing international, Inc.
5900 Green Oak Drive
Minnetonka, MN 55343
1-800-328-3895

President/CEO: David D. Murphy
Vice President/Editorial: Patricia K. Jacobsen
Vice President/Retail Sales & Marketing: Richard M. Miller

BIG-BASS SECRETS
Executive Editor, Outdoor Group: Don Oster
Editorial Director and Project Leader: David R. Maas
Senior Editor: David L. Tieszen
Managing Editor: Jill Anderson
Creative Director: Brad Springer
Senior Art Director: David W. Schelitzche
Art Director: Joe Fahey
Photo Researcher: Angela Hartwell
Production Services Manager: Kim Gerber
Production Staff: Laura Hokkanen, Kay Swanson

Contributing Photographers: Mark Davis, Paul Duclos, Jr., Jerry Gibbs, Bob McNally,
Rich Zaleski

Contributing Illustrators: Chris Armstrong, John Dyess, Steve Stankiewicz

Cover Illustration: "Largemouth Bass with Cattails" by Al Agnew

Contributors: Pure Fishing (Berkley)

Printed on American paper by: R. R. Donnelley & Sons Co.

10   9   8   7   6   5   4   3   2   1

Library of Congress Cataloging-in-Publication Data

Big-bass secrets : catch trophy largemouths and smallmouths with the
  experts of Outdoor life.
        p. cm.
    ISBN 0-86573-111-X (soft-cover)
    1. Largemouth bass fishing. 2. Smallmouth bass fishing. I. Title: At head
of title: Outdoor life. II. Creative Publishing International.

SH681 .B54 2000
799.1'77388–dc21   99-056908

Table of Contents

Introduction

If you're the gambling type and bet on large and smallmouth bass as the most popular freshwater critters in fins today, you'll win. Not only are these all-American gamefish found in every state except Alaska, but they've been introduced around the globe to European and African countries, Japan and beyond. Since the late '60s they've spawned an entire tackle and boat industry through fishing competitions and dedicated bass angling organizations. There's not a bass angler I know who can get enough information on the sport, and that's where *Outdoor Life's Big-Bass Secrets* comes in, targeting the kind of specialized info you need to catch big bass wherever they swim and whenever you fish.

Here you'll find the most authoritative voices on the sport, writers like Mike Hanback, Rich Zaleski, Jimmy Dean, Larry Larsen, Bob McNally, Will Ryan and the Bass Professor himself, Doug Hannon, zeroing in on the two keys to bassing success—knowing where to find fish, and then getting them to eat. In the section "The Right Place at the Right Time," you'll find season-long strategy to ferret out both bass species from any cover or structure in lakes, reservoirs and rivers during problem conditions from high water to difficult cold fronts. And you'll learn that scorning some long-held beliefs can lead you to bass others miss.

Once you have Mr. Bigmouth and his high-jumping small-jawed cousin cornered, you need to play the music that turns them on. Section two, "Triggering Strikes," does just that. You'll learn tricks for using the major bass lures in new and unconventional ways—just the ticket for hard-fished waters—and why some little-used artificials and natural baits often work even better. From techniques of winning pros to stealth approaches for fish others think are uncatchable, there are tactics that will ring the bell in your home waters. Keep *Big-Bass Secrets* in a handy place; it's going to become your best single source for fishing success in the seasons to come.

Jerry Gibbs, Fishing Editor, Outdoor Life

The Right Place at the Right Time

Bass Profiles

by John E. Phillips

It doesn't matter what type of bass you target, these fish provide the ultimate angling experience.

TO SUGGEST THAT BASS ARE THE most celebrated freshwater fish in America today is no exaggeration. Songs and countless numbers of books are written about black bass, and fortunes are made, and lost, catching them. The relentless pursuit of bass has resulted in some anglers losing their jobs, their families and even their peace of mind.

What is it about the bass that causes such an angling craze? The answers are many, but mainly it's the characteristics embedded in the fish's genetic makeup—their elusive, fierce-battling and high-leaping nature—that creates an addiction among anglers.

So let's take a closer look at the bass family, from the granddaddy largemouth to the lesser known Neosho Smallmouth. These brief profiles of each species and subspecies offer insight into bass behavior, indicate where you'll find bass and why you fish certain ways to catch them, and provide other interesting and entertaining facts about the nation's most popular gamefish.

Largemouth Bass

(Micropterus salmoides)

A native of North America, today the largemouth bass (above) is found in all states except Alaska. Apart from its often pot-bellied appearance, the largemouth's most distinguishing feature is, not surprisingly, its big mouth. The upper jaw extends past the eye, making for a massive maxilla that accounts for the fish's trademark fierce and accurate strike.

The fish spawn in the spring or early summer, as the male clears a nest in the soft bottom and entices the female to lay her eggs. In about a week to 10 days, the eggs hatch. The bass fry that survive—often only 10 to 40—usually mature in 3 to 5 years.

Across most of the United States, largemouths (also known as bigmouths, widemouths, green trout, hawgs and bucketmouths) seldom weigh more than 5 pounds. However, in Southern lakes with longer growing seasons, largemouths weighing more than 10 pounds are common. One such Southern lake yielded the current world-record fish, a 22-pound 4-ounce monster caught on June 2, 1932, from

Georgia's Montgomery Lake by George W. Perry. The last large-mouth catch to threaten the world-record mark came from California, and the majority of line-class records presently recognized by the International Game Fish Association (IGFA) also were taken from this state. For these reasons many bass authorities believe that California holds the next world record. However, trophy large-mouths, many more than 18 pounds, are now found in most of the Southern states from Florida to Texas.

Of course, many anglers and biologists are convinced that the next record largemouth will not come from a major reservoir but rather from a farm pond somewhere in the Deep South. Farm ponds usually are heavily fertilized, have very little fishing pressure and often provide habitat for bass to grow older and bigger than major reservoirs do.

Florida-Strain Largemouth Bass

(Micropterus salmoides floridanus)

In recent years, the biggest stir in bass fishing has been caused by the Florida-strain largemouth, which apparently grows faster and survives longer than the northern strain. Stocked in waters nation-wide, the Florida-strain largemouth has accounted for more lake records being broken and more state records being raised than any other single factor.

Smallmouth Bass

(Micropterus dolomieui)

The smallmouth bass is more streamlined in appearance than the largemouth, is bronze in color and has distinct red eyes in some areas. The smallmouth does not have the largemouth's lateral stripes, but often has dark bars running vertically along its sides. Often called bronzebacks, brown fish and tiger-stripes, smallies are easily distinguished from largemouths because the fish's upper jaw rarely protrudes past the eye, as it does with its gape-mouthed cousin.

Smallmouths favor cool, running water in streams and rivers, or clear, rocky lakes, and cannot tolerate warmer water. The fish tend to remain in lower depths, except when feeding, and they typically hold next to rock shelves, gravel bottoms and big boulders.

In most of the smallmouth's range—from Minnesota and Quebec

SMALLMOUTH ARE WILLING BITERS AND STRONG FIGHTERS—two traits that make them the favorite species of many anglers.

south to northern Alabama, then west to eastern Kansas and Oklahoma and other states where smallmouths have been introduced—the average fish is 2 pounds or less. However, fish more than 7 pounds are caught frequently on the Tennessee River in Kentucky, Tennessee and Alabama. The spread of smallmouths is a direct result of the nation's railroad system. Until 1869, the smallmouth's range was confined to the Lake Ontario and Ohio River drainage systems before railroad men carried them to other parts of the country.

The world-record smallmouth weighed 10 pounds 14 ounces and was caught in 1969 from Dale Hollow Reservoir in Tennessee. Most smallmouth bass prognosticators believe that the next record fish will come from the Tennessee River, where most of the biggest smallmouths have been regularly caught.

SMALLMOUTH BASS (top) have a jaw that extends only to the middle of the eye, rather than beyond the rear of the eye, as in the largemouth (bottom). Because of the difference in mouth size, smallies usually strike smaller lures than largemouths do.

Neosho Smallmouth Bass

(Micropterus dolomieui velox)

The distinctive Neosho subspecies is more slender than the smallmouth and lives in the Neosho River and its adjacent tributaries of the Arkansas River in Oklahoma, Arkansas and Missouri. Because of dams built in the area, the Neosho smallmouth has a limited range today. The velox in the Neosho's scientific name means swift, which refers to the fish's most exciting trait.

FACTS ABOUT BASS

▲ **BLACK BASS ARE FRESHWATER FISH** but not true bass (Serranidae). Black bass are actually members of the sunfish family (Centrachidae), which includes crappies and bluegills. The three major species of black bass are largemouth, smallmouth and spotted bass. Redeye, Suwannee and Guadalupe bass are secondary strains of black bass. White bass and stripers, including the saltwater and freshwater fish, as well as hybrids, belong to another family—the Percichthyidae.

▲ **BASS ARE PREDATORS** and will eat almost anything that falls in the water, including snakes, lizards, worms, crayfish, other fish, frogs, insects and even their own young. Bass feed erratically but most often at dusk and dawn. Approaching storm fronts, the availability of schools of baitfish, intense light and moon phase all seem to influence when bass feed.

▲ **BASS HAVE KEEN EYESIGHT** and can distinguish between colors. They see well underwater because of the curved shape of their eye lenses, which allows five times more light to enter the fish's eye than a human's eye and also gives bass excellent peripheral vision.

▲ **BASS ARE COLD-BLOODED,** therefore water temperature plays an important role in the life of the fish. Until the water reaches 60°F or so, bass generally are not active, as the cold slows down metabolism, digestion and the nervous system.

▲ **A MUCH-TRAVELED SPECIES,** bass were spread across the United States by a variety of means, including in the tenders of coal trains, in railway fish cars, by hand, on canal barges and tractors, in milk cans, polyethylene bags and specially equipped tank trucks. Bass have even been transplanted successfully to Europe, Africa and Central and South America.

How to Catch the Biggest Bass in Any Lake

by John E. Phillips

Tournament pros reveal the secret spots big bass use to avoid the average angler.

―――――――――――

WHILE HUNTING DEER FROM MY tree stand last year, I learned that tree stands are one of the most productive places on earth to ponder the deep mysteries of life. It's then that you're high above the earth and free to meditate away from ringing telephones, loud music and people with nothing to do but interrupt your work.

It's there that a sportsman can try to solve the mysteries of things such as: Where do the trophy bucks stay, and how can a hunter take them? How do you decoy a flight of hunter-shy ducks? How do you find the biggest bass in any lake?

Never having been able to locate the biggest bass in any lake, I decided that to find that fish, I might be able to use the same strategies that a detective would utilize to find a missing person. He would begin by interviewing everyone who knew that person intimately. He would talk to the people who'd had business dealings with him, and he would gather information from the people who'd spent the most time with him.

As the detective interviewed and talked to those who knew the missing person best, a pattern of that person's habits and haunts would become evident. Then, to locate that missing person, the investigator would look in the areas where the person would most likely be. If, through interviewing the ones who knew him best, the detective discovered hideouts that the person had retreated to in the past to dodge danger or elude pursuit, then the investigator could reasonably assume that that person would use one of those sanctuaries again. I decided that the tactic I would employ to find the biggest bass in any lake would follow these same guidelines.

My first source of information on how to find the biggest bass in any lake was Rick Clunn of Montgomery, Texas, four-time winner of the B.A.S.S. Masters Classic and 1988 B.A.S.S. Angler of the Year. Clunn has seemingly developed a sixth sense for finding bass that, combined with his years of fishing experience, makes him an expert in the ways of bass.

"I have found that on any lake there are pressure zones, which are created by boat traffic and fishing pressure," Clunn explained. "Big bass avoid these zones just like trophy deer keep away from areas where the hunting pressure is the heaviest. The fish that will react quickest to fishing pressure or boat traffic are the larger fish, particularly bass weighing 8 pounds or more, because they have learned to survive by dodging human pressure and have become the biggest fish in a lake.

"An angler must study the lake, the fishermen and the baits most often used to pinpoint the high-pressure regions. Then you'll know the target sites where many sportsmen are fishing and the depths of water that most of their baits are covering. For instance, visible targets like points that look as though they will hold bass, trees and bushes close to shore are places any bass fisherman will point out and say, 'I bet bass are there.'

"However, I search for areas to locate big bass—like an isolated stump well off the bank that you only can find by crashing a crankbait into it. I also look for a segment of water where baits are not being run through. If most anglers are fishing deep-diving crankbaits or plastic worms, which cover the bottom story of water, and buzzbaits and topwater lures, which run along the surface, I will fish a medium-diving crankbait, which passes through the middle story of water. This area is obviously not getting any pressure, so it should be where the big bass are holding.

"One of the reasons why the flipping technique produces so many big bass is that even though a zone receives a lot of fishing pressure, a big bass can find sanctuary in that same region in the thick cover. A bass may be holding so tight in the cover that the only way to catch the fish is to flip a bait through the densest part of the cover where the bass has not seen any lures."

With Clunn's information, we can mark a lake map and eliminate the pressure zones where large bass are not likely to be. By eliminating parts of a lake, anglers shrink the area where they'll have to search for large bass, just as detectives searching for a missing person discard places where they know the person who is missing won't show up.

Next, I talked with Hank Parker, of Denver, North Carolina, a two-time B.A.S.S. Masters Classic champion and B.A.S.S. Angler of the Year in 1983. Parker believes that when a bass grows larger than 4 pounds, the fish has eliminated all of the predators that have threatened its life except one—the angler.

"Therefore, I think a bass that's larger than 4 pounds realizes that in the presence of man, it becomes the prey," Parker explained. "So, a bass of this size hides from and avoids areas where it will encounter the supreme predator, man. I've learned that big bass that have been unmolested are far easier to catch than bass that have been pressured by anglers. So, search out sites that receive very little fishing pressure even if the spot doesn't look as though it will hold a bass. A bass on a small, solitary piece of cover is more likely to take your lure than a bass of the same size that's holding on obvious cover that sees 20 or 30 lures a week.

"Although big bass will sometimes hold on obvious cover in high-pressure zones, these fish are very difficult to catch. Often, the only way to get a lunker that's positioned on obvious cover to bite is to stay well away from the cover and make one accurate, long cast to that cover instead of four or five casts. Make sure that the lure swims perfectly and naturally by the cover and doesn't intimidate the fish. To catch a big bass in a high-pressure zone, you can't beat the water to a froth with your lures."

As I talked to Parker and Clunn, I began thinking about that day in the tree stand. The information I gathered from Clunn and Parker was almost identical to what hunters realize is required to harvest a trophy buck. A sportsman must search for trophy deer in overlooked areas where a deer feels very little, if any, hunting pressure, and he must approach the animal with the utmost caution and care so that he won't spook the deer. That's exactly the formula proposed by Parker and Clunn to take the biggest bass in a lake and it's the same one that a detective would use to find a missing person.

According to Jack Hains of Zwolle, Louisiana, who won the B.A.S.S. Masters Classic in 1975, hunt for areas that no one else would choose to fish.

"I take numbers of big bass on clean banks that don't have any cover or structure," he said. "Most fishermen look at these areas and say, 'There's no point in fishing that spot because there's no reason for a bass to be in that place.' Although there may not be but one or two bass in a half-mile of clean bank, those couple of bass usually will be larger bass that are very aggressive because they haven't seen many lures.

"Another place where I find bigger bass is on the deep tips of long points. Because most anglers fish in the top 5 to 8 feet of water on a long point, that zone is the story of water that receives the most fishing pressure, boat traffic and wave action. All of that pressure on the baitfish and bass causes them to move out onto the deep end of the point. Although very few anglers fish the deepest tip of a point before it drops off into a creek or a river channel, that's the place where I usually find the bigger bass."

So, I learned that by fishing longer and more intensively in what appears to be nonproductive areas, a fisherman may be able to catch bigger bass.

Just as a detective might consult human behavioral scientists to determine what a particular personality type might do under stress and pressure, I talked with a fisheries scientist, Ken Cook of Meers, Oklahoma. Cook searches for big bass as a professional angler and was the winner of the 1983 Super B.A.S.S. Tournament and the 1991 B.A.S.S. Masters Classic. I knew that Cook could tell me why large bass do what they do and base that information on sound, scientific principles.

"Big bass like their solitude," Cook said.

"By the time a bass reaches its trophy potential, it probably has had some negative experience with anglers. Therefore, it has learned how to avoid fishermen.

"Big bass prefer to hold where there's some type of overhead cover, which can be either heavy structure or deep water. A big bass becomes very territorial-minded if it finds a piece of heavy cover that it can stay in without being harassed; often spending much of the day in that cover while relatively inactive. The only way to catch a large bass like this is to put a bait close to the bass. Even though the fish is a large bass, it's still an opportunistic predator that will attack any bait that passes close by.

"If the big bass is not in heavy cover, the fish will generally go to deep water," he continued. "Bass that are deep are very hard to catch because an angler can't place his lure as accurately in deep water. He can't see the structure where the fish is holding. Accurate lure presentation can trigger an instinctive bite from a large bass that may not want to feed. But most fishermen are not as proficient with lures in deep water as they are in shallow water."

Denny Brauer, 1987 B.A.S.S. Angler of the Year and 1998 B.A.S.S. Masters Classic champion, from Camdenton, Missouri, says, "To

RELEASE A BIG BASS rather than killing it for "the wall." A good photo and an accurate measurement is the perfect way to record the moment forever.

catch a big bass, I've got to get my boat into an area where no one else would consider putting his boat. I must cast my lure into a spot that only a nut would try and fish, because those are the regions where you will find big bass. I've jumped beaver dams with my boat to get into protected water where no one else can fish. I've run my boat across sandbars at the mouths of creeks where the sheer force of the motor pushed the boat across what was almost dry land. If you can reach an area that no one else can fish, you may discover that big bass of a lifetime.

"And don't be afraid to lose some baits. The type of cover you must work a lure through to take big bass may cause you to lose lures. To catch a lunker, a trophy angler must outfish all of the other fishermen who are trying to take that same bass."

Although most anglers agree that big bass are often in out-of-the-way, hard-to-get-to places, unlikely spots such as swimming areas also may hold big bass. Because there is so much splashing and carrying on in a swimming area, most fishermen never cast a lure around beaches or roped-off swimming sites when they're not in use by bathers. So often this is an overlooked, productive region to find big bass.

Some bass anglers have been successful fishing around boat ramps, because just about every lake in the nation has at least one tournament on them each weekend. The big bass that are caught from the lake and brought into the weigh-in site are usually released at the boat ramp and nearby boat docks. The largest stringer of bass (75 pounds 9 ounces, 21 bass) ever turned in at a B.A.S.S. Masters Classic was caught in 1984 on the Arkansas River by Rick Clunn, who found the bass on a small, obscure ledge not far from the boat ramp where the anglers put in their boats.

George Cochran, in the 1987 B.A.S.S. Masters Classic on the Ohio River at Louisville, Kentucky, caught his winning stringer of bass close to the put-in place. Most of the other anglers who had participated were traveling a couple of hundred miles per day to reach prime fishing areas and spent only 2 or 3 hours fishing each day.

Another place to look for big bass is in ponds that nobody fishes. Once, I caught an 8-pound largemouth out of a gravel pit right next to a major highway that thousands of anglers passed each day while traveling to a nearby lake. A big bass may be in a location so public that no one thinks to fish for it there, including golf course ponds, which receive little or no fishing pressure and may be home to trophy bass.

Now that I had narrowed down my search pattern as to where a big bass should be, like any investigator, I next needed to know how to confront or capture the one I sought. Larry Nixon of Hemphill, Texas, is not only a B.A.S.S. Masters Classic winner and two-time B.A.S.S. Angler of the Year, but also one of the best anglers in the nation on determining what will make a big bass bite.

"Two of the reasons why more fishermen don't catch more trophy bass is that they either fish too fast or don't fish with large enough lures," Nixon explained. "A trophy bass fisherman must be willing to not catch a bass at all in a day, because he's using tactics and baits to take only big bass. Big bass like large lures presented slowly. And those big baits cull the large numbers of fun-catching, smaller-size fish. Slow, deliberate angling for the biggest bass in any lake isn't as exciting to most anglers as fishing fast and covering lots of water."

After developing a system to search for and possibly take the biggest bass in any lake, I realized that to implement the system, I would have to forfeit some of the sheer fun that bass fishing for all sizes of bass provides.

So, if a trophy fish is your goal, you now know how to find and catch it—by slowly fishing large lures in hard-to-fish places or by fishing the spots where no one believes there are bass. Often, these anglers are the ones who will go home with the catch of a lifetime.

The Dock Side of Bassing

by Neil Ward

Catching bass doesn't require locating stumpy drop-offs and grass beds, as anglers discovering bassing's dock side are now seeing the light.

THERE IS A UBIQUITOUS form of cover on lakes and rivers around the country that many fishermen keep ignoring in their search for likely bass hangouts. Though anglers diligently watch their depth finders for signs of stumpy drop-offs or submerged grass beds, far too many anglers fail to appreciate the fishing importance of the numerous docks that now line most major reservoirs and rivers.

It is a mistake that is keeping a lot of bass anglers from catching more fish because docks create excellent cover for bass, especially on aging bodies of water where most of the natural cover has eroded away. By learning how to effectively fish docks, an angler can go to almost any lake or river in the country and catch bass.

Fred Chivington, an engineer and former bass fishing guide who lives in Welaka, Florida, has used his dock fishing savvy to boat limits of bass from New York to Florida. Because he knows how to fish docks, Chivington is usually able to quickly formulate a bass-catching pattern, even on unfamiliar waters.

When most bass fishermen imagine fishing in Florida, they envision casting plastic worms into quiet coves covered with lily pads, not pitching lures underneath towel-draped docks in people's backyards. But a few hours in the boat with Chivington would be enough time to to change anyone's mental image of "bass cover."

"I catch plenty of bass on the St. Johns River by fishing docks,"

Chivington said. "On the river as well as on other Florida waters, bass regularly gather around the man-made cover created by docks."

Docks are definitely great places to catch bass. But just like other forms of cover, every dock doesn't hold a fish. To successfully fish a dock pattern, an angler has to determine which docks are most likely to produce bass so that he or she can eliminate dozens, perhaps hundreds, of unproductive docks.

Sometimes, the material that the dock is constructed from is important. Chivington has discovered on the St. Johns that docks with concrete posts are more likely to attract bass than docks with wooden posts. He believes that the reason for the preference is because algae and other aquatic life readily collect on the porous surface of a concrete post, and this attracts more baitfish.

Some of the newer docks have piers made from concrete-filled plastic pipes, which are created by driving plastic pipes into the bottom and then pouring concrete inside the hollow pipes to make them solid. In the process, there is often excess concrete that spills into the water and forms a rough patch of rubble near the base of the pipe. Chivington has discovered that bass often lie on or suspend over the patch of misdirected concrete.

In addition to the materials that a dock is made from, the season of the year often determines where a bass will set up residence around a dock. In the spring, bass will probably be under the runner (the walkway leading to the dock), where the water is usually shallower. Shallower water warms up faster, and if the bottom is suitable, bass will spawn around the posts supporting the runner. "During the spring, the first posts on a runner that are situated outside of the eel grass [which often covers a shallow bottom] will normally hold a spawner," said Chivington about St. Johns bass.

As the summer arrives, bass will often hold underneath the main body of a dock not only because of the vast amount of shade and cover that it provides, but also because the dock usually sets in deeper water than the runner. Understanding how bass relate to docks, Roger Farmer of Dalton, Georgia, will fish docks more than other types of cover in the hot summer months. "In the summer and early fall when the air temperature hovers in the 90s, I head for docks instead of deeper creek channels and points, where most summertime fishermen go," Farmer explained.

Farmer likes to fish docks in hot weather because he has found that

DOCKS are the perfect location for largemouths to find both security and food.

he can catch some thick-bellied bass from underneath the overhead structure. "I may not catch as many bass as some fishermen who are fishing deeper, but I catch bigger bass," Farmer said. "And when I get a bite, I like for it to be something that can stretch my string."

Farmer dissects a dock by flipping a jig or plastic worm into every possible place a bass might hide. When he gets a strike, Farmer notes where it occurred, and if he gets a few more strikes from similar locations on other docks, he knows that he has discovered the locational pattern for the day. Then he will confine his flips and pitches to the productive areas only, as he fishes dozens of docks during a day's time. "Some days, the bass will be way up under a dock. And other times, they'll be on the outside edge or maybe under the ladder," Farmer explained.

Fred Chivington has found that when two posts are closer together than the other pilings on a dock, many times bass will be between the two posts. He believes that because they are closer together, the two posts make the bass feel more secure.

Another favorite hideout is where a dock joins a runner to form a "T." The "T" creates an irregular feature that attracts bass.

Bass also prefer the older, more dilapidated docks over the newer ones. And isolated docks are better for fishing purposes than a string of docks because bass have fewer places to hide and are thus easier to locate.

Probably the one ingredient that improves a dock's appeal to bass more than anything is the presence of brush. A dock that has sunken brush around and underneath it is always a better choice for bass than a debris-free dock. On most lakes, fishermen can usually find a few docks that are owned by other fishermen who have "improved" their docks by sinking brush around them. Anglers should make special note of those docks because they will produce bass on a consistent basis.

When fishing an unfamiliar lake, Chivington will usually run a paper graph recorder as he casts to docks. By leaving the graph running, he doesn't have to constantly gaze at the screen to spot sunken brush. Instead, he just occasionally checks the paper printout for signs of submerged brush.

A dock's location in relation to underwater structure is often the major reason why it is productive while other docks in the vicinity are not. For example, anglers may catch two or three bass from the outside posts on a wooden dock and think that they have discovered a pattern. They then may fish three or four similar docks and come up with blanks, even though everything appears to be the same. But if they enlarge their scope of vision, they may suddenly see more than just outside posts on wooden docks. For example, they may discover that the productive dock was located near a point and that the other docks were back in a bay. If this is the case, the fishermen should immediately head their boats toward a wooden dock on the opposite point and proceed to catch a few more bass.

"I've seen it happen many times," said former Santee Cooper bass guide Carl Maxfield of Summerville, South Carolina."I may fish a dozen docks without a strike, and then catch three or four bass from one dock. When I do, I then analyze the spot, and a lot of times, the dock will be near a change in the lake's bottom, such as a point, creek channel bend or ridge."

So anglers should always remember to not concentrate so hard on the dock itself that they forget to take into consideration the lake's topography where the dock is situated.

Though docks produce bass all over the country, all docks are not built the same. Fred Chivington took his Southern dock-fishing skills to the Thousand Islands of New York, and there he caught bass around "cribs." With the heavy ice that covers northern waters in the winter, people can't build docks with conventional wooden posts because when the ice breaks up in the spring, it would rip the posts out. To solve that problem, dock owners build wooden boxes from railroad ties that are called cribs. They fill the cribs—which may measure 8 x 8 feet—with rocks, and they use several cribs to form docks that will withstand the pressure of moving ice. Chivington has found that bass relate to the cribs just as they do to conventional docks.

Chivington's favorite lure for fishing a dock, whether it's in Florida or Canada, is a 6-inch plastic worm paired with either a $\frac{1}{8}$ or $\frac{1}{16}$-ounce slip sinker. He pegs the slip sinker onto his line with a rubber band. (Unlike a toothpick, a rubber band won't nick the line.) Pegging the sinker allows him to skip the plastic worm several feet underneath a dock because the lure and sinker stay together when he makes a hard, sidearm cast.

Chivington uses a 5$\frac{1}{2}$-foot, heavy-action spinning rod paired with a spinning reel and 10-pound-test line for most of his dock fishing. The short, powerful "dock rod" allows him to cast, skip and pitch a plastic worm into every conceivable hiding place that a dock creates. "A spinning outfit allows me to make casts that I wouldn't be able to make with baitcasting equipment," Chivington said.

Once he skips a plastic worm underneath a dock, Chivington may let it lie there as long as 30 seconds before he moves it. A lot of times, a bass will pick up the worm as it rests motionless on the bottom. When he gets a strike, Chivington sets the hook with a quick, strong snap of his wrist, and he hopes that this will get the bass' head pointed toward the boat. He then sweeps his rod sideways and tries to drag the bass out from underneath the dock before it can tangle up his line.

If a bass does hang him up, Chivington doesn't pull and tug on the 10-pound-test line. Instead, he just keeps a tight line and waits for the bass to swim out. It doesn't always work, but Chivington has found the wait worthwhile on several occasions.

"Sometimes, I'll flip a dock using heavy line, especially if the water is real dingy or the wind is blowing, reducing the visibility in the water," Chivington said. "But most of the time, I prefer to stay back from a dock several feet and cast to it using a spinning outfit and lighter line."

The productivity of his method was never more obvious than during a bass tournament that Chivington fished on Florida's Lake Eustis. His partner didn't fish with spinning equipment and lighter line because he wanted to flip to the docks with heavy tackle. They flipped to one series of docks for 30 minutes without catching a fish. Chivington then backed the boat away from the docks a short distance and skipped a worm. He proceeded to catch four bass from the same docks to which they had just finished flipping.

Besides plastic worms, Chivington also likes to fish crankbaits around docks. Bass often chase baitfish that congregate around docks, so Chivington likes to pitch and skip a lightweight balsa crankbait, such as Normark's Shad Rap, underneath docks and bump the crankbait off the piers. A crankbait bouncing off the wooden structure is often more than a bass will tolerate.

Carl Maxfield likes to fish topwater lures around boat docks that have lights affixed to them. "Early in the morning, a big bass will often be around a dock with lights," Maxfield explained. "Lights attract insects and schools of minnows during the night. And at daylight, I have tangled with several bass weighing more than 5 pounds that were chasing minnows around a dock."

When an angler catches a bass from a dock, he should be sure to make several more casts to it because docks are one form of cover that will hold more than one bass. In fact, Fred Chivington has caught as many as 15 bass from beneath a single dock!

To catch more bass from today's heavily developed shorelines, anglers should learn how to fish docks. And if they do, they may never go searching for a stumpy drop-off again.

Bad Water Bass

by Jim Dean

Tired of fighting crowds at the local hotspot? Well, the best place to catch a truly lunker largemouth might be the most miserably managed water you can find.

NEARLY EVERY SUMMER FOR AS long as I can remember, Curtis has backed the John Deere into the marshy cattails along the water's edge and hooked up the pump. Poised on the bank, the rig reminds me of some giant mosquito with its flexible probe sucking the life out of the pond. Aluminum pipes stretch into the surrounding crop-lands, and by mid-July half the water is in the rows.

With the mud flats baking in the sun around a dwindling, muddy puddle, it's not a place that invites you to fish. Even when it's full, you can cast from the bank at only a couple of openings in the nearly impenetrable thicket of encroaching willows, alders and cat brier. And after nearly 30 years of neglect, the pond contains textbook overpopulations of stunted bluegills, paperthin crappies, green sun-fish, warmouths, golden shiners, bullheads and whatever else Curtis and his father might have tossed in over the years.

A half-mile down the dirt road is another pond built more recently. It's bigger, more accessible and carefully managed. As a result, it yields sassy, slab bluegills that average nearly a pound. No soda-cracker crap-pies, no shiners, no competition for food. The bass are smallish, but numerous and willing. It's the kind of pond that makes anglers drool and fisheries biologists proud. Of course, that's where I always fish.

That's also where I was headed the warm spring afternoon I stopped as a courtesy at the barn to let Curtis know I was there. He was stand-ing outside speaking to his neighbor, who was holding a fishing rod.

"Broke it clean," the neighbor was telling Curtis.

"Busted what clean?" I asked.

"Busted my line," said the neighbor. "It was a huge bass. I got a glimpse when he come to the top. It ain't the first time, either, but I'm not equipped for 'em."

"I've never caught a big bass in there," I said.

"He's not talking about the new pond you always fish," said Curtis. "It's that old irrigation pond on up the path."

"You're kidding," I said, astonished.

"No I ain't," said the neighbor. "That new pond's got big bluegills and a lot of bass, but most of the bass are small. If you wanna squeeze about a half-dozen of those bass into one real handful, you've been fishing the wrong pond.

"Of course," he added with a grin, "you've got to get 'em before it gets hot and Curtis starts laying pipe."

It didn't make sense to me, nor was I sure that I believed him, but not many fishermen can ignore that kind of tip. That afternoon, I passed up the pond with the big bluegills and slid my 12-foot aluminum boat through the brush into the old pond. The water was dingy as usual, but at least it was bank full. Curtis wouldn't begin irrigating out of it for at least another month. I began to cast a plastic worm under the old willows that had grown up around the bank.

I caught only three bass, but they were eye-openers. The first weighed nearly 5 pounds; the second was more than 3. As the sun dipped below the trees, I cast the worm into the top of a pine that had fallen into the deeper water along the dam. It was promptly inhaled by a largemouth that tipped my hand-held scales at 7 pounds. I drove home that evening happier than usual, but with more questions than answers.

What sort of biological turnabout was going on here? Why would an old, neglected pond containing a population of stunted panfish produce such good bass fishing? And why, especially, were the bass I routinely caught from that nearby well-managed pond seldom bigger than 2 pounds? Was it just luck—an isolated incident—or had I stumbled onto something more significant?

It's no secret that fishing the right kind of water is the most important key to quality bass fishing. After all, you can't catch lunker bass where they aren't, and it doesn't matter what you use or how you use it. And like most fishermen, I have always assumed that a well-managed body of water would fit into the "good bass fishing" category. It seems so obvious. It's also, as I have since learned, sometimes very misleading.

What do we know about the kind of water that grows big bass? Most fishermen are well-acquainted with the cycle that takes place on newly impounded waters. In most cases, the bass fishing usually peaks sometime between the fourth and seventh year, then gradually declines. Lots of sizable bass will be caught during that peak period, and a fair number of true whoppers will continue to be caught for a few more years. After about 10 years, however, the average size of bass tends to drop considerably, and lunkers become the exception rather than the rule. Older lakes and ponds occasionally recycle over the years and experience brief periods of improved fishing for various reasons, but such cycles are unpredictable and that first decade of fantastic fishing is seldom repeated.

For this reason, many fishermen concentrate on lakes that are experiencing their peak years. It's a good idea. But if that's all they're doing, they're overlooking a heck of an opportunity.

This spring, when you get tired of fighting the mobs on your favorite hot lake, it's time to look for the kind of spots most bass fishermen ignore. In fact, you should actually seek lakes and ponds that are long past their prime—spots that have a reputation for stunted panfish and too many rough fish such as golden shiners. It might be an ancient, neglected puddle like that pond I described earlier, but it could also be a local city water supply lake, millpond or similar body of water. Chances are it will not be terribly large—a couple of thousand acres at most—and more likely less than 100 acres. It may be a backwater oxbow along a river, or a neglected pond long ago abandoned to kids who are delighted to catch runty panfish on cane poles. You aren't likely to catch a lot of bass in such a spot, but you'll almost certainly have a better chance at catching a few bigger bass, maybe even that double-digit largemouth.

In recent years, Jack Avent and I have regularly fished such spots. For one thing, we enjoy the lack of competition and the more leisurely pace, but that's not all. We've been catching more big bass. One of our favorite spots is a millpond with a stone dam built by hand a century ago. Its headwaters are pretty badly silted, and dense grass beds hide legions of small panfish and minnows from the relatively few bass. The bass population is limited by the silted spawning sites and also because the smaller fish rob nests each spring, keeping the bass population in check. Yet those bass that do manage to survive the first year have an incredible source of food that's just right for growing heavyweights.

Every season, Jack and I catch bass in the 6- to 8-pound class out of this lake, and we know of a 13-pound county record that came from it. On a steamy afternoon last summer just before dark, we were fishing the lily pads alongside of what's left of the old shallow creek channel.

"Sometimes just before dusk, big bass will move up this cooler channel and ambush passing bait from the pads," Jack remarked as we cast topwater lures into likely openings. "I've had my best luck fishing ahead of the boat in the channel or along the edges."

A few casts later, Jack cast a Hula Popper beyond some lily pads and began an erratic, gurgling retrieve. When his lure reached the pads, a bass weighing nearly 8 pounds inhaled it in a massive boil and almost immediately jumped, trailing behind pads and stems. It was pure calendar art, and after a few anxious moments, Jack lipped his prize and swung it aboard.

"I wouldn't trade a bass like this caught on top water in these classic surroundings for a dozen 3-pounders from some huge impoundment," he said as he released the fish. Nor would I. It's one of the more tangible reasons for fishing neglected waters.

One very important point to remember about old lakes and ponds is that though they may be neglected and unmanaged, you want to make sure that the ones you fish are reasonably fertile. Avoid lakes that are too acidic to grow big bass. You can test this with a pH monitor, but in all likelihood, your best clue will be word of an occasional lunker largemouth caught by kids or old-timers fishing for those runty crappies and bluegills.

There are biologically sound reasons why many old, neglected bodies of water often yield bigger bass than some well-managed small lakes and ponds.

A few weeks after I landed the trio of fat largemouths from that old irrigation pond, my son Scott and I fished a pair of large, well-managed panfish ponds, and my long-held beliefs took a direct hit—one that seems tied to my experience in ways I had never noticed before. Both of these prime ponds have received intensive management designed to produce big bluegills and shellcrackers. And do they ever produce!

Using crickets that day, three of us caught at least 60 panfish ranging from 14 to 33 ounces. By late afternoon, I began to notice swirls, slurps and showers of tiny minnows erupting in the shallows.

"They're bass feeding in there," said our host, Cliff Edwards. "There's a pile of them in here, but these ponds don't produce many big bass so I don't think you'll be interested."

"Speak for yourself," I said. "We're going to get into the other boat and try 'em." During the next 2 hours, Scott and I caught about 40 of those feeding largemouths on a variety of lures. It was great fun, yet not a single one of those fish exceeded 2 pounds.

As we loaded our gear that evening, I asked Cliff if he had any theories that might explain why all those bass were small, especially because the pond was rich in food and old enough to produce big bass. After all, I noted, the bass we'd caught seemed healthy, and there were certainly plenty of them. Why weren't there more big ones?

"I think it's simple, really," Cliff replied. "I know it's hard to believe, but there's actually not much food in here for bass after they reach about 2 pounds."

"That doesn't seem possible," I said.

"Sure it does," said Cliff. "With all the fertilizer we use, there's plenty of small food and forage for little bass and all these big bluegills and shellcrackers. But there are virtually no rough fish in these ponds except channel catfish—no shiners, suckers or any of the other long, soft-finned forage fish that bass really prefer. So the panfish grow very fast. That means that there are relatively few midsize fish of any kind in here. These smaller bass can't eat a bluegill that weighs nearly a pound or more. It takes a whopper largemouth to do that, so there's a wide gap in the food supply.

"After a bass reaches about 2 pounds in one of these well-managed ponds, it needs those medium-size fish to eat, and we don't have enough of them."

What Cliff described is a piscatorial Catch-22. There's plenty of food for a lunker that could eat a bluegill the size of a pie plate, but few bass ever reach lunkerhood because they can't find enough of the right food to get past the 2-pound mark. It makes sense in a twisted sort of way, but when I asked fisheries biologists if it were possible, they readily admitted it is not at all unusual.

"Most sophisticated pond management techniques are geared

toward producing panfish, and that doesn't always benefit bass," one biologist told me. "In fact, the more intensely you manage a pond for panfish, the more likely you are to create a food gap that can prevent many bass from reaching large sizes." He also added, however, that this situation applies mostly to smaller lakes and especially ponds and is less common in really large lakes where intense management is not as practical.

As for old, neglected waters such as those I described earlier, biologists have also learned that they can hold some surprises. Jimmy Davis, a former fisheries biologist with the North Carolina Wildlife Resources Commission, recalled a modest-size lake he and his assistants had to drain.

"As expected, it had a huge overpopulation of rough fish and stunted panfish, but only a few bass," he said. "There were a few small ones, but most of the largemouths we gathered were 5 pounds and bigger. There weren't a whole lot of them, but enough to make it worthwhile for a skilled and patient fisherman. With so much food they were hard to catch, and I doubt many fishermen even knew they were there."

All of this should give you some ideas, of course, but if you go after lunkers in smaller, neglected waters, there are some general tactics

you should follow. Your quarry is a well-fed, wary old mossback so you should use lures, tackle and techniques for big, solitary fish. I prefer casting tackle with 16- to 20-pound-test line because these waters often contain lots of stumps, grass and other cover. Deep-diving crankbaits and other big-impoundment lures will work, but because the water isn't as deep, you'll find them less useful. Instead, your best bets in the early spring will be spinnerbaits and jig 'n pigs fished along the dam, edges of channels or around points near deeper water. Because the water warms more quickly in these smaller lakes and ponds, and because you'll find bass in the spawning shallows much earlier, shallow-diving minnow imitations and even topwater lures will get action. A topwater buzzbait can be a killer from the early spring through the entire season, and it's a big-bass favorite. As warm weather arrives, I stick pretty much to weighted plastic worms, and because I'm after big fish, I like worms at least 7½ inches long.

It's especially important to fish at dawn whenever possible because lunker bass in these old lakes and ponds are particularly tough to catch during full daylight. Dusk is almost as good as dawn, and both are prime times to try topwater lures. One of the most effective tactics is night fishing with a noisy surface lure such as a muskie-sized Jitterbug. In some of these neglected spots, it's one of the surest ways to bag a big bass on an artificial lure. Only one other enticement is likely to be as effective in these waters, and that's a large, live shiner.

Just because you're fishing smaller water doesn't mean that you should leave your modern electronics at home. A trolling motor, thermometer and depth finder (you may need a portable model) will give you the same edge here as it does on big impoundments.

You won't catch a lot of fish, but it only takes one bass to make a lifetime memory if it's the right bass. My guess is you'll take that memory from some miserable mudhole you wouldn't have given a second look. Until now, that is.

Bass Before the Buds

by Jerry Gibbs

Just after ice-out and just before pre-spawn, bass will mosey on into the shallows to catch some rays. I'm there with them each year to catch a few bass.

WE WERE ON THE WAY TO A trout river when we began passing the reservoir.

"Stop!" I said suddenly. I couldn't help it. "Let's just go see a minute."

Roger Cole yanked the truck into the access road to the lake. It was just after ice-out, and though the weather had been warm I knew that the water of the big reservoir had barely reached 50°F. It was not what you'd call for if fast bass fishing was on your mind. Still, I just had to stop and see. You know how that goes.

Roger parked the old pickup with the still older canoe tied in it, and we walked down to a rocky point that thrust into the reservoir. The point marked the start of a sheltered deep-water cove. We stood looking down into the clear, sunlit water and spied the shapes of carp milling about on the protected side of the point. But they weren't carp. We said it simultaneously and not very quietly: "Bass!"

Why were they here so soon? It was far too early for spawning, and not the right kind of place, either. It was even too early for so-called pre-spawn movements when bass head in from deeper water, holding at various locations and different depths until stable weather and rising temperature signals their rush for the bedding grounds.

We didn't know why those bass were there and really didn't much care at that point—but we were back at the truck fast, trout trip on hold, churning down to a launch site to put in the canoe. Besides fly tackle all we had was trout-oriented light spinning equipment. No official bass stuff. There were tiny jigs, in-line spinners, ultralight spoons, small balsa minnow plugs. It would have to do. There was no way we were going to leave all those fish in peace. The trout gear would do awfully well as it turned out. It was also a wild introduction to perhaps the most unpredictable part of the bass season—the ultra-early spring.

We caught fish—largemouths, not smallmouth bass—in the deep-water cove, near the point on the protected side. We caught more we could not see. They were near logs and large rocks that broke the monotonous regularity of steep shores in places outside the cove. There were some fish holding where riprap had spilled during the bank stabilization process to form little rock pile buildups out from shore. The protected areas were best. The irregularities in them proved to be the key. Two days later when we checked there was not a bass in any of these places. It figured.

From extremely early spring through spawning, bass go through a series of rapid-fire behavior and location changes that make the back-springs and hoop-jump tricks of trained circus dogs look as exciting as octogenarian aerobics by comparison. Here's how it works.

The season's first stretch of bright, warm spring days (warm, sunny days following ice-out in the North) often result in a brief flurry of inshore bass movement. In deep reservoirs such as the one in which my angling companion and I did so well, the fish move close to steep rocky or clay shores. This gives them deep water close at hand for quick exit when the weather sours. Time and again I've seen groups of bass on such shores, their backs just below the surface. It's almost as though they're soaking up the first warm rays of sun before their bio-clocks begin the countdown to spawning. I've seen them in a scant 2 feet of water basking like this, but almost always there's a drop to more than 10 feet of water close by.

I used to choose only small ponds and lakes for my very early bass fishing because they warm earlier due to their shallower, smaller physical makeup. Small lakes are definitely a good bet this time of year. But then I learned about big-lake inshore fish movement. Each large lake or reservoir is slightly different. Each will have a handful of specific spots that experience this early activity. The only other consistency is that the action is short-lived and very much dependent on day to day weather.

The water during these early fish movements will typically be clear—both of tint and vegetation—and that makes use of certain lures not only possible but preferable. That reservoir surprise my pal and I tapped is a good case in point. Our aborted trout safari and the quick press into service of small lures we had on hand was good fortune. That day and trips since have proved that in-line spinners such as Mepps, Panther Martins or Rooster Tails are some of the better lures on barely active early bass. Because you don't have to contend with heavy vegetation or moss now, the exposed hooks on the in-line spinners are rarely a problem. If there's a lot of brush or underwater obstacles in the area, I'll use one of the Mepps Combo Killers with a single Keeper hook and a weedless-rigged plastic tail. The No. 2 is 1/8 ounce, and I sometimes drop to the 1/10-ounce, No. 1 blade rig. The high-quality in-lines will spin even at slow speed, which is how you want to retrieve them.

Inshore, "sunbathing" bass also respond to light, floater/diver minnow plugs (Rebel, Storm, Cordell, Bomber, Rapala and so on). Cast them past promising fish-holding areas and twitch them slowly on the retrieve. Use split shot to keep these plugs working just under the surface. In more snag-filled areas, tiny Beetle Spin or other spinnerbaits aimed at panfish are excellent lures. Also try small 1/8 to 1/16-ounce leadhead jigs dressed either with plastic or marabou for fish that are closer to or on the bottom. If there is any of that so-called slime moss on the bottom, you'll have to keep jigs swimming above it. In this case I'll often use tube jigs, sometimes suspended beneath a float, pulled and danced at a set level across likely areas.

Since the inception of tournament fishing, many bass anglers have grown up totally without concept of the most effective means to take inactive, ultra-early bass—natural bait. Except in specific regional areas in the country, it's just no longer traditional to fish natural bait for bass as it is for panfish, northerns, walleyes, saltwater species and in some cases trout. In fact, standard walleye techniques are potent on early bass, and unless you've fallen asleep and let a largemouth totally swallow a natural bait, all fish can be released as easily as when using a bare man-made bait.

For bottom-oriented fish, try a simple plain jighead with half of a night crawler or a lip-hooked minnow on it. Bass slightly off the bottom, suspended higher from the bottom, or in very shallow water, can be enticed with a variety of walleye rigs. Included is the venerable slip-sinker rig. Use the bent-beanshaped Walking Sinkers for gravel or rocky areas, bullet weights where more snags or young vegetation prevails. Use a bit of cork or a floating jighead on the snell or leader attached to the hook to keep the crawler or live minnow suspended at desired levels.

Another simple natural bait rig is a floating jighead with split shot clamped 18 to 24 inches ahead of it on the line. Hook a lively minnow on the floating jighead. For bass you suspect are suspended not far beneath the surface, try a slip bobber, which you can adjust for any depth. Hook up a minnow or crawler, and clamp some split shot on up the line to keep the minnow at the desired level and to keep it from swimming to the surface and tangling around the float. All bottom-oriented sinker rigs should be worked by raising them, pulling them forward with the rod, then reeling up slack. If you're good with plastic worms, you'll be good with these rigs. The trick is keeping the bait near bass. They often take awhile to respond during this time of year. You can use the natural offering as a locator, then switch back to artificials if you like.

Remember bass researcher Doug Hannon's northwestern factor when searching for these early bass. Hannon's advice to fish northwestern corners and shores because they are the first to warm was misunderstood by some anglers who went charging off to the northwestern end of a lake or reservoir. The northwestern shore or northwestern cover could be in a cove or bay in the east or south or west of a lake. The point is, you are looking for areas that have a *southern to southeastern exposure* because with the sun in that quadrant now, those exposures will feel its full effect—especially in Northern latitudes. You may also want to look for areas where the bottom composition is darker, thus more light/heat absorbent than lighter areas.

All these things mean only subtle differences, but they are enough to result in bass being present or not. And even then, don't expect great success every time you try for the early fish. They will flee like thieves in the night as fronts slide in, the sun hides, and temperatures again drop. The next phase in spring bass movements can produce some beautiful action. The fish respond to more expected techniques and lures.

The terms "pre-spawn" and "staging" bass have been talked about a lot. They've come to mean certain things on different waters. New anglers coming along sometimes get the impression that all of the bass in a lake are ganged up at a kind of submarine starting line ready to charge en masse for the spawning grounds. Well, in a way, that's right. Lengthening days and warming water bring bass to biological spawning readiness. But not all fish spawn at once. If they did, the year-class of young would stand a far poorer chance of survival. Nor do all of a lake's bass hold at one launching place before moving onto the spawning grounds, which themselves are typically widely located about the water body.

What we have learned is that every year bass tend to hold at certain kinds of places before moving in to spawn. It all depends on what's available in the lake or reservoir. In the very simplest description, they move from deeper water to the shallows. What is important is to understand the specific deeper water structure or cover type. Edges are one key.

Bass move in from underwater main river or tributary channels where those exist, and hold on the edges of the channels. They also move to the edge of a shore's first major drop or break into deeper water. They can be at the ends of long underwater points, the edges of deep dormant weed beds, the deeper edges of standing timber ridges or humps in deeper water just off any of the afore-mentioned places. If man-made objects are present in deeper water close to spawning areas, the bass will use them, too. Given fairly stable water temperature, the fish will concentrate in these kinds of places throughout a lake and become more susceptible to good presentations.

Of course, on large water bodies with many suitable spawning areas and different exposures, bass will be in pre-spawn concentrations at different times, which means that you can lengthen this productive fishing period. Pro angler Ricky Green goes high-tech to do just that, using his maps and depth sounder to locate the key areas and then employing one of Lake Systems Combo-C-Lectors to monitor light, temperature and pH in fishing spots where combined conditions are most favorable. On new and large lakes when time's at a premium, it's the fast way to lock onto the hot area of the moment. Take "hot" literally, too.

Ripe bass that leave staging areas and attempt to spawn in the shallows are as affected as those early nonspawning fish by sudden weather shifts. Even before they begin actual bedding, bass cruise the vicinity first. They'll be in bays and smaller coves, holding around stumps, remains of old weed beds, docks, logs and rocks. Let the sky darken, the temperature drop, the wind pick up and they'll fade back to deeper water, though it seems to me not as quickly as in little ponds and lakes. It may be only briefly before they're back. Let a real front pass and they'll remain in the deeper water even longer. Here's some good news, though.

Often the larger bass choose slightly deeper water in which to spawn. During weather shifts of short duration, they may not be as affected as the shallow-water fish. Also, if you can tough it out dur-ing a miserable spring cold front with raw temperatures and chilling rain, you'll frequently do very well fishing the deeper staging areas.

Bass in staging areas like channel edges, the secondary points before creek channels or the creek channels themselves, and they will still take lures during horrible weather—especially the bigger fish. Afterward, during cold and high pressure, they can become somewhat tight of jaw, to say the least.

One of the prime staging areas during these shifts to poor weather are weed beds. Bass here are likely to hit through the worst of weather. Many anglers who relate to and fish visible weed beds later in the season totally forget about them now. True, there's no sign of the thick verdant growth that may explode on and through the water surface later, but things are beginning to happen underwater. Just as the fish themselves have ripened, vegetation—especially in Southern regions—is beginning to grow. Brown and once seemingly dead beds even 15 feet down are sending out green tendrils. Snag a crankbait down there. If your hooks come up with even a little greenery, you've probably hit a prime staging area.

Those short duration shifts from hot to overcast cold weather won't always push fish directly from the shallows in larger water bodies. Fishing with one of New Jersey's top bass anglers, Rocky Ventone, we had already taken one good fish from a bridge support in the center of a channel leading to a protected backwater sector of the lake. Rocky felt that a lot of fish were holding in similar deeper areas now, ready to move back where they'd already been during a freak hot spell a couple of weeks earlier. The thing was, they hadn't vacated those shallows at once.

"It was crazy," Rocky said. "It was 90°F. Then the temperature went down a little for a day or so, then it really bottomed out and it rained for a good week. The worst thing that happened was in a tournament.

"I fished a stump field in about 4 feet of water on Saturday before the tournament and didn't catch a fish there. It was already clouding up, then it turned cooler and by Sunday the guy who won the tournament did it in the stump field. I think the bass had been even shallower than that field, and didn't all run right to deep water. I think a lot of them stopped at those stumps because the wood was still a little warm from all the sun. Then the next day it got really cold and stayed cold and they moved all the way back to the deeper water. But we're on a warming trend again. Some of those fish gotta be out of the deep water by now."

They were. Rocky and I caught them back in natural coves and one seemingly man-made cove that connected to the main lake via a nar-

A JIG-AND-PIG is a deadly lure on bass staging outside traditional spawning bays.

row boat canal. We found them moved tight to man-made objects—mainly docks and retaining walls. Here the water ranged from 2° to 4°F warmer than the main lake. That's all it takes. A sudden shift to cold weather that lasted more than a day would doubtless send them to the deeper channel of the small boat canal. Longer than that and they'd slip back to the main lake. Any time the weather deteriorates during the spring, look for the fish first in deeper water nearest to the area bass were using when they moved inshore.

Fishing concentrated pre-spawn bass in various staging areas can be easier than when they've moved in and spread out just before nest building. The lures will be much larger than those suggested for bass that made those first inshore warm-up visits. In the deeper staging areas, weedless jigs trimmed with pork, imitation pork (like Dri Rind), jigs and plastic eels or tails, are all effective for the biggest fish. Work them with a slow lift-drop movement of the rod tip. Add big-blade $3/8$-ounce or larger spinnerbaits slow-rolled deep for bass of mixed size.

As bass move shallower and spread out before spawning, a combination of baits, both large and small, become effective. What to use depends on water depth, clarity and aggressiveness of the fish. Choose $1/4$-ounce spinnerbaits as one of the best water-covering lures. Lipless vibrating plugs (Cordell Spots, Rat-L-Traps, Fin Manns) are good, too. Slowly retrieved floating minnow plugs are effective for less aggressive fish. Sometimes small surface baits and fly-rod poppers will provide action that will surprise you. Add to the list suspending plugs such as the Arbogast Arby Hanger and Rebel Spoonbill Minnow, which can be worked almost in place once cranked down. Use plastic tails or plastic worms on a $1/8$-ounce jighead. Swim them rather than work them in standard lift-drop fashion.

In very shallow water, try unweighted plastic worms with or without a little split shot ahead on the line. Flyfishermen have a choice of rabbit-fur/deer-hair fly lures in both diving head configuration or with weighted eyes to take them down. They enter the water very quietly and are excellent in the extreme shallows as well as slightly deeper water.

Bass also spawn around tall emergent grasses, maiden cane, bulrushes, cattails or so-called pencil weed and normally hold at the edges of the deepest growing of this vegetation just before moving in. Frequently this will be at the mouth of a slough, cove or larger bay. First, though, they move to any irregularity along the deeper edges of the vegetation. Cuts, pockets, little points, minibays, all attract them, as do detached ministands of the weed away from the main bed. If there is additional nonemergent vegetation there, so much the better.

Bass can't push back into truly dense cattail stands as they can in reeds and cane. Instead they utilize undercuts caused by current or other phenomena. Typically a bank of thick cattails will have only a few undercuts deep enough or with additional adjacent cover—a rock, log or pocket—to attract spawning bass. You can usually spot the better places by getting close to the bank at its end and looking parallel down its length.

Spinnerbaits are fine searching lures for emergent vegetation, as are jig-rigged swimming worms, plastic lizards and plastic crayfish. You can work the plastic baits a lot faster than you normally would in deeper water. If the midsize lures strike out, try experimenting again with the very small baits you used on those ultra-early warm-up bass. Once again, try the mini-spinners and spinnerbaits; perhaps a panfish-size minnow plug. And don't forget those crappie-size marabou jigs when the fish are just about ready to spawn.

Coaxing nest-guarding bass and getting them to respond once bedding is over requires a whole new set of tactics. And that is another tale. Meanwhile, keep your eye on the local bass waters in the very early spring, even if you are in trout country. And remember, what at first looks like carp may not be carp at all.

Exploding 10 Bass Myths

by Larry Larsen

Extensive studies by fisheries biologists have blown many common bass myths out of the water. Test your own knowledge of bass fact or fiction.

A NGLERS ARE SOMETIMES HOPE-lessly gullible, prone to take myths about bass as gospel. Yet evidence from fisheries biologists often tells a different story. Today, most fishing fiction pertains to bass behavior, their feeding and spawning interaction and environment. However, scientific studies are now exploding many of these myths.

One biologist leading the way in setting the bass record straight is Wes Porak, the largemouth bass project leader for the Florida Game and Fresh Water Fish Commission in Eustis. Porak has spent years studying the largemouth bass and its habitat, and his research has refuted many so-called facts regarding how the bass interact and react to their environment and environmental pressures. The following are 10 of the common myths and misconceptions about bass—and the actual realities—according to Porak's extensive biological research.

WILL FISHING FOR LARGEMOUTH BASS during the spring spawn have a detrimental impact on the success of the spawn? Many biologists say no.

MYTH: *Fishing during the spawning season impacts the success of the spawn; if everyone fishes a particular lake and removes spawning bass, the bass population will be decimated.*

REALITY: Fishing does not impact the spawn or the number of fish that are actually produced in a given year, according to numerous studies. These studies have shown no relationship whatsoever with the number of spawning fish in the lake and the actual outcome or success of that spawn for that given year. The success of a spawn during any given year is always primarily related to the quality of the habitat available. By all accounts, therefore, actual fishing during the spawn—as much as it goes against the grain of some anglers—does not affect the spawning process.

MYTH: *A small area of structure usually holds only one bass, so if you catch a fish, you should move to another area.*

REALITY: Fisheries biologists have found through sampling that large numbers of fish will concentrate on just a small amount of structure. In fact, anglers who do catch a fish in isolated areas of structure should continue to fish that spot for at least 5 minutes.

MYTH: All bass move from offshore deep water to the inshore shallows to feed, and then back out to deep water after the meal.

REALITY: Although some fishery studies have documented fish moving inshore in early morning hours or in the evening, there have been more studies that have proven that other bass just won't do that. Fish have individual behavioral patterns. Some bass are more sedentary and tend to stay within a small area, while others, call them "wanderers," tend to move a great deal. One study on a non-vegetated lake in central Florida revealed that some bass are consistently found on the shoreline, while others basically stayed in offshore areas all of the time. The truth is that a certain segment of the bass population is comprised of offshore fish that don't come into shoreline areas.

MYTH: Rising water levels just after the spring bedding season can negatively impact the success of the spawn. As a result, the bass population will be down the following fall and worse the next spring.

REALITY: As stated earlier, the spawn is typically affected by two things: the amount of aquatic plants in the lake and the water level.

AFTER CATCHING A SINGLE BASS in an isolated area of structure, keep fishing. Chances are more largemouths are holding in the same structure.

BIG BASS are reputed to eat only big forage. In reality, bass usually feed on the most abundant forage they can find—even miniscule minnows.

When water levels rise during the late spring and into the summer, strong year-classes of bass are typically documented throughout the Southeast. Flooded areas of habitat allow young bass fry to be more productive in predation. As a result, the population in the fall will be greater and, because of the ample forage, the bass larger in size.

MYTH: *When big bass are placed in a live well, such as in tournament situations, and carted several miles away to be released, the fish will remain in that new spot. As a consequence, the area they were removed from will be depleted.*

REALITY: Behavioral studies using radio-telemetry or fish tagging have found that big bass have a homing instinct. Bass typically have a home range and tend to spend the majority of their life within that area. When you move a bass several miles, very often it will return to its home area.

MYTH: *As long as bass are released during the spring, we can catch and keep our limit the rest of the year, without affecting the fish population— even on a small lake.*

REALITY: Heavy fishing pressure, with anglers limiting out and taking too many bass at any time of the year, may hurt the fish population. You can overfish a lake, particularly a small lake, in any season—summer, fall or winter. Also, it's much easier to affect the fishery in a very small 20-acre lake than in large, natural fisheries. Bass anglers should be conservation-minded year-round.

MYTH: *All bass prefer to feed on the largest forage they can get into their mouth, so anglers should throw large lures at all times. A 15-inch bass, for example, will always eat food items the size of your favorite 3/4-ounce lure.*

REALITY: The size of forage is related to the size of the bass going after it, however, keeper-size bass in the 12- to 15-inch range are frequently found with very small food items in their stomach. That's true especially in vegetated areas where there may be a tremendous abundance of small forage items like tiny minnows and grass shrimp. The same holds true in waters where threadfin shad are present. If the shad have a good spawn, you'll find a lot of 3-pound bass eating shad that are less than an inch long. If fishing is slow, go to a smaller lure. For example, Porak was checking creels recently when he came across a panfisherman who was using the tiniest jig on the market. He had more keeper-size bass in his cooler than all of the seven or eight bass boats on the lake.

BASS FEEDING HABITS are dependent largely on water temperatures and size of prey. Large forage may actually take several days to digest.

MYTH: *Bass, like people, feed daily, and they consume and digest about the same amount of forage each day. Some time during that day, the bass will feed, so catching them is simply a matter of staying out on the water and fishing until the dinner bell rings.*

REALITY: That's not the case with cold-blooded animals, particularly when water temperatures are cool. The digestive system of a bass is related to the water temperature—the warmer it is, to a point, the faster the fish digest their food. Obviously, the quicker bass digest their food, the more frequently they feed. In very cool temperatures, the fish may only feed once every few days. Feeding activity also has to do with the size of the prey being consumed. If a 7-pound bass, for example, consumes a ¾-pound chub sucker, the fish may sit and digest that for 3 or 4 days.

MYTH: *Bass grow fairly rapidly in Southern waters and reach 12 inches in about a year. Fishermen normally call 1-pound bass "yearlings."*

REALITY: Growth studies by fisheries biologists in the South have shown that a 12-inch largemouth might be anywhere from 2 to 3 years old. The average yearling bass will be around 6 to 7 inches in length. There are tremendous variations in growth, so you may actually find year-old bass that are just 3 inches long and others as big as 14 inches. Both are exceptions to the norm.

MYTH: *A 12-pound bass caught just after the spawn probably would have weighed 3 to 4 pounds more had it been caught before dropping its eggs.*

REALITY: Many studies have shown that weight loss caused by spawning is much less than commonly believed. In fact, ovaries taken from trophy bass have been studied extensively by biologists. The actual ovary only weighs from 2 to 8 percent of the body weight of a bass. It is largely water, with limited actual tissue mass. Typically, the ovaries of a 12-pound bass during the spawn wouldn't weigh more than about a pound.

Magnifying Bass

by Michael Hanback

*Despite their size, small waters
give up big bass and fast action.
Here's how to cash in.*

———————⤳———————

ONE SPRING THREE FRIENDS AND I held a mini-bass tournament in the backwoods of Mississippi. We paired off in johnboats, cranked up the electric motors and hummed away to fish the flooded timber.

First off, I zipped a black worm to some structure and twitched it back. Bang! A 2-pounder hammered the bait and began to put up a scrappy fight. Bang! Even as I played my fish, another bass smashed my partner's spinnerbait. A double, what turned out to be only our first of the day, was on.

A hoot rang out from the far end of the pond, where our competitors, with grins on their faces, reeled furiously.

We met at the landing 2 hours later to compare scores. Among us, we caught more than 60 largemouths, including several 3 pounders. We called the tourney a draw, filleted the few bass we kept and returned to camp to enjoy a Southern fish fry. The water we had fished was all of 10 acres. Tops.

Next time you drive by one of those little ponds, or an ugly flooded strip mine, or along a narrow stream, take a second look. A long second look. Then try to find a way to gain access. Often those small waters, those unremarkable little gems, hold big bass and fast action.

In these days of crowded, high-pressure fishing, there's a lot to be said for these overlooked waters. They're easy to get to. You don't need an expensive boat or an armload of rods, just your favorite spinning outfit or baitcasting rig. You can fish from the bank, wade or use a float tube to probe these pockets of great bass habitat. Amid the peace and solitude of these spots, you can cast to unpressured bass with elbow room to spare. With hundreds of thousands of man-made ponds and lakes throughout the country, most of America's 13 million bass anglers have convenient access to such water. Best of all, you can catch and release 20, 30, even 100 fish a day. Many bass will run from 8 to 12 inches, but these miniature fisheries yield plenty of big bass each season—largemouths to 11 pounds, and smallmouths that tip the scales from 3 to 6 pounds.

Ponds

Many bass ponds, typically 1 to 10 acres in size, are located on farms and ranches. Others, such as the one we fished in Mississippi, are nestled in wetlands or woodlands. Golf courses, resorts, sporting preserves and other commercial operations are often laced with ponds and they may offer access.

But often such tiny waters are unknown even to nearby residents. One way to discover ponds is to pay a visit to the courthouse. There you can examine plot, planning-commission and soil-conservation maps for the precise location of ponds. As a bonus, you also learn who owns them. Find the owner, and you can often get permission to fish. Fish and game agencies can also provide brochures, maps and other information for accessing small waters.

When prospecting for ponds, keep in mind that many are initially stocked with largemouth bass and largely forgotten. If adequate cover, forage and oxygenated water are available, and if bluegills are kept in check, those "neglected" ponds produce fair to excellent angling year after year. But the death knell for many ponds is the heavy buildup of silt, weeds and algae, as well as an overpopulation of stunted bream (which eat bass eggs). Don't think that just because there's a splotch of blue on a county map, you've discovered the ultimate honey hole—it is just a tip as to where to look. A little scouting will tell you the rest.

Ponds that are either managed commercially or privately by landowners can offer some of the finest largemouth fishing in America. Evidence of this is clear at The Great Outdoors, a nature and golf resort in Titusville, Florida, where 20 of its 2- to 5-acre ponds are stocked with bass.

"When we started managing these ponds years ago, we brought in 3 pound bass to spawn," says Jim Conley, wildlife manager at the resort. "We also planted aquatic grasses and established shrimp and other forage for bass."

In Florida, bass can grow a pound per year—particularly when they get a catered smorgasbord.

"We regularly catch 5- to 10-pound bass by fishing from docks or from the shore," says Conley. "Last February, a friend of mine caught an 11-pounder in one of the little lakes we manage."

Golf courses, resorts, and sportsmen's lodges often have similar action. Access to these waters is restricted, and you'll probably have to pay to fish them. But it's worth shelling out a few bucks once in a while to battle bass in these made-for-lunker habitats.

A few simple strategies can maximize your success on any pond. First, be stealthy. Ease along the edge of a pond, much as a trout angler would approach a stream or pool. Use weeds, cattails and other shoreline cover to break your outline. Big bass in little places are skittish.

Working from the bank at dawn or dusk, cast into shallows rimmed with weeds, trees or other cover where bass hunt for minnows and insects. Docks, drainpipes, flooded timber, brush piles and fallen logs are where both bass and baitfish congregate. Fish these areas with plastic worms, shallow-running crankbaits or thin-minnow plugs.

In the heat of summer, you must fish deep, which usually means getting somewhere near the middle of the pond or by a dam. Consider slipping into a float tube or launching a canoe. A johnboat equipped with an electric motor is best for ponds 5 acres or larger. Fin, paddle or motor quietly to where you can probe drop-offs, creek channels and other depths.

SLUG-GOS are the perfect lure for tempting smallmouths in shallow streams.

Streams

Virginia, where I live, is laced with smallmouth rivers, such as the famous Shenandoah and the James. So where do I go when the fishing heats up beginning in June? To a couple of secret, out-of-the-way streams.

I can throw a rock across these waters in most places, and wade them in summer without getting my shirt wet. With the current lapping my calves, I enjoy the solitude and the area's wood ducks, whitetails and bald eagles.

I also catch smallmouths, lots of them. Fifty on a good day of fishing. In the clear, shallow streams, the bass are at their predatory best, hammering lures with explosive power.

Once a strictly eastern fish, smallmouth bass have been successfully stocked across the United States. If impoundments and large, cool-water rivers with moderate gradients in your region hold healthy populations of the smallmouths, chances are, nearby streams will also offer good fishing.

For largemouths, seek out the warm, slow-moving streams that curl through farm country, marshes and other flatlands. On streams where water temperatures and cover are conducive to both species, large-mouths and smallmouths often coexist.

Angling a stream begins with reading the water. Largemouths are usually found in deep, still pools with structure, while bronzebacks prefer swift water littered with rocks, riffles and gravel bottoms. But nothing is gospel on streams, that's why they can be so alluring. Each summer, I catch smallmouths at noon on 90°F days during feeding frenzies. Or while probing foaming, rocky eddies with plastic worms or grubs, I also take the occasional largemouth. Bass in streams are simply where you find them.

Wading is a great way to canvass a bass stream. The combination of wading and canoeing is the ultimate because it allows you to cover up to 8 miles or so of water each day. Float-fish awhile, then beach your canoe and wade to prime fishing holes. On streams, as in all lit-tle waters, the fish are easy to spot since the limited habitat concentrates bass around obvious structure.

For fast action, cast plastic worms, Slug-Gos or spinners into shady water laced with weeds, rocks or logs. Work weighted worms or medium-running crankbaits through deep pools and lazy stretches where big bass hang out.

Bass face upstream or perpendicular to the current while waiting for minnows, crayfish, adult insects or nymphs and other foods to drift into range, then they shoot out to nab them. Casting lures slightly upstream and working them down through the pockets of water will trigger the most strikes.

TACKLING LITTLE WATER

▲ **FOR BASS IN LITTLE PLACES,** choose a medium-weight, graphite baitcast or spinning rod 5½- to 6½-feet long. Spool baitcast reels with 8- to 14-pound-test monofilament, and spinning reels with 8- or 10-pound line. I often go light when fishing clear, shallow streams in summer and fall. A 5½-foot graphite stick and matching spinning reel with 6-pound line is perfect.

▲ **SMALL- AND MEDIUM-SIZE LURES** best imitate the bass forage found in ponds, streams and pits. Stock your tackle box with a good selection of shallow-running crankbaits (I prefer crayfish and minnow imitations) and black-and-silver Rapalas.

▲ **TRY ¼-OUNCE GREEN, YELLOW AND WHITE SPINNERBAITS** in ponds and pits. You can catch a lot of 8-inch stream bass on Mepps, Panther Martins and similar inline spinners of various colors, though I rarely hang big fish on these lures.

▲ **AT DAWN AND DUSK,** you can prompt explosive topwater action with Jitterbugs, Tiny Torpedos and other plugs. Use compact plugs on tiny ponds and streams, and larger, louder lures on big ponds and pits where lunker bass may prowl.

▲ **PLASTIC WORMS MEASURING 4 TO 6 INCHES LONG** and rigged with either one or two hooks are dynamite for largemouths in all small waters. Carry an assortment of black, purple, natural and motor-oil colored worms.

▲ **BLACK, PURPLE AND PUMPKINSEED COLORED GRUBS** measuring 2 to 4 inches in length are also excellent choices, as are 3-inch black, silver and metallic Sluggos. I regularly catch smallmouths during the day by twitching these crippled baitfish imitations on or just beneath the water's surface.

Pits

Abandoned coal, iron, phosphate, lime and gravel pits can be gold mines for anglers. Many strip mines, blasted and bulldozed from the earth years ago, then flooded, harbor good numbers of largemouth bass. The areas where deep pits are fed by cold-water springs or creeks are often home to smallmouths.

If you live in an area where strip mining was employed, check out these abandoned and reclaimed pits. Get topo maps and aerial photographs of the old mines. You can save a lot of time studying those maps for flooded timber, rock structure, deep water falloffs and other prime bass cover.

GRAVEL PITS are ideal locations to find largemouth bass.

From an angler's perspective, pits are similar to ponds. You can fish them conveniently from the bank, or use a float tube or small boat. Work cover-rimmed shallows at dawn and dusk, and cast baits to deep channels, drop-offs and ledges during midday.

While some pits are honey holes for bass, others are devoid of fish. The only way to find out for sure is to get out there and probe them with lures, or call a biologist or nearby tackle shop to get the scoop.

Wayne Gendron deer hunts on property in northern Missouri that has a network of abandoned coal mines. Reclaimed pits, most of them 50 yards wide and 100 yards to a ¼-mile long, dot the lease. Gendron knew that the Missouri Conservation Department and a few independent landowners had stocked some of the pits years ago, but he had never taken the time to fish them.

"Last September a friend and I were putting up deer stands, but it was just too hot to be walking in the woods," Gendron says. "We decided what the heck, let's see what's in those pits."

Gendron knew that the few pits near a major highway already received moderate fishing pressure, so he and his friend packed float tubes into pits only a few hundred yards farther in.

"It was scary, the number and size of the bass in there," Gendron says. "It was obvious the fish hadn't seen a lure in years—if ever. They hit small spinnerbaits and hammered Rat-L-Traps. Some big bass spun our tubes around like tops."

Tubing and fishing from the shore, Gendron and his partner caught and released more than 100 largemouths that day. "We had a scale and several bass were 5 to 7 pounds. My partner caught an 8-pounder," he says. "It was unbelievable, just awesome fishing in those little places."

The Spawn's Early Bite

by Doug Hannon

It's never too early to think bass–the largemouth spawn is coming soon to a cove near you.

THERE'S ALWAYS A CERTAIN MAGIC in largemouth bass fishing. But never is it more enchanting than during the springtime spawn. Maybe it's the visual element of this yearly spectacle, the fact that you can *see* the bass holding brazenly over their nests in the shallows, challenging all intruders. Or maybe it's the sheer aggression of the fish—even the typically reluctant lunkers—which prompts them to strike everything thrown their way.

Simply put, the spawn is a time of suspended reality, a time when sight-fishing for big bass—in predictable, shallow places at foreseeable times—is not only feasible but it's fantastically productive.

That much, most fishermen know. But this annual alchemy is a complex mixture of behavioral elements. Here's the breakdown.

The spawn is triggered by length of day, moon phase and, chiefly, water temperature. Once the water reaches the low 60s in early spring, egg-laying begins immediately following the next full or new moon. In the Deep South, the event can occur anytime from February through April. Once it does, the spawn gradually migrates north.

LARGE FEMALE BASS are often willing biters just before the spawn.

The rule of thumb holds that for each day, the spawn moves 17 miles north, which works out to about 500 miles per month. So while the spawn may occur in Florida in March, in Tennessee it begins in April or May, and in Michigan it happens sometime in June. But whenever the spawn kicks in, the behavior that accompanies it is as predictable and frantic as a Wrestlemania bout.

Spawning's Early Changes

Approximately 3 weeks before observable nesting, when the water reaches 55 to 60°F, bass segregate themselves by sex and start to exhibit "staging" behavior. Female bass, the larger of the species, gather in great numbers over underwater points that reach into greater depths, particularly near the mouths of spawning coves and bays. Here they vigorously rub their sides and bellies against the bottom or any firm structure in an attempt to dislodge parasites, an activity known as "glancing." It's as if the fish know that the unusual amount of sunlight they will be exposed to while they're on the nest in the open shallows promotes the rapid growth of fungus and parasites, which can cause serious infections.

For the angler, finding one of these staging points in 6 to 12 feet of water is a bonanza. Large female bass can be caught in great numbers, as new fish constantly move in to the points to replace those filtering out to bedding areas. On *extremely* calm days, staging areas can be detected by underwater flashes of light from the sides of the fish and

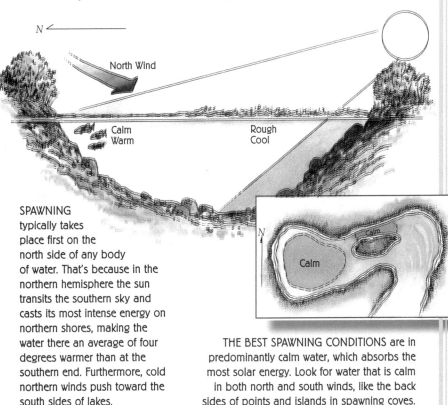

SPAWNING typically takes place first on the north side of any body of water. That's because in the northern hemisphere the sun transits the southern sky and casts its most intense energy on northern shores, making the water there an average of four degrees warmer than at the southern end. Furthermore, cold northern winds push toward the south sides of lakes.

THE BEST SPAWNING CONDITIONS are in predominantly calm water, which absorbs the most solar energy. Look for water that is calm in both north and south winds, like the back sides of points and islands in spawning coves.

by large, subtle boils reaching the surface. (Remember to mark these spots. The same staging areas will be used again after breeding, and will remain productive for several weeks after the spawn while the fish slowly disperse to their summer haunts.)

While the females are staging, the male bass can already be seen in the shallows acting as if they are defending eggs on a nest. In point of fact, these fish haven't built the nest yet, but are testing the security of the area by chasing out every bluegill, minnow and other threat to their eggs, an activity they'll engage in for up to 2 weeks before actually building the nest. If they can't maintain a protected perimeter, they'll find another place to spawn.

Needless to say, these extremely defensive males are easy to catch. However, I would question the ethics of doing so since they're engaged in an activity that drives the entire spawning system.

Bed Making: A Male Activity

By the time the water temperature in the shallows reaches 60°F, the males have begun fanning out shallow nests that appear on sandy bottoms as light-colored circles. They'll typically build these nests in 2 to 6 feet of water, in places where a thin layer of silt blankets a firm bottom. The firm bottom is key, but the males are also looking for a textured surface where the eggs can find purchase—a tuft of grass, for example, or gravel—any nook or cranny that will provide anchor and protection for the eggs. If they can't find a firm bottom, the fish will make do on a large lily-pad root, the top of a stump or log or even the fork of a standing tree.

Eggs on the Nest

When the water reaches 65°F, the last of the females will have moved into the shallows to await the final spawning trigger—the moon. The morning after the next full or new moon brings one of nature's true spectacles. Huge black-eyed, turquoise-shaded females list on their sides and proceed to deposit their eggs into the nests like dirigibles unloading ballast. Meanwhile, the smaller, golden-toned, orange-eyed males alternately release their fertilizing milt and, nose to the sky, mix things up with the greatest thrust their tails can muster. The process continues for 8 to 36 hours, during which the fish are so singleminded they're impossible to catch.

It's often erroneously said that the female bass plays a minor role in

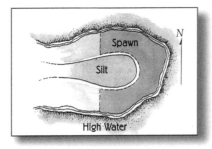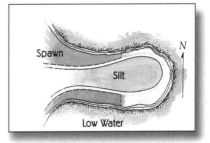

THE RELATIVELY STILL WATERS of a spawning bay or cove allow a greater buildup of bottom silt than in open lakes. Because the silt layer is thicker farther back in the cove and precludes nest building, bass spawn on the cove's sloping edges, where the bottom is relatively stable. But they do so as far back in the cove as possible, where the calmest, warmest water is found. Water levels determine exactly where that is. In high-water conditions, bass spawn in the back ends of the cove, where the water has encroached upon firm terrain (left). But in low water, they'll spawn high on the banks of the front half, the warmest, calmest firm-bottomed waters in the cove (right).

defending the nest. The truth is, soon after the eggs are laid, the posture of *both* fish turns defensive. The male hovers over the clutch of eggs, while the female pulls back to the edge of the bed. By her formidable predator presence alone, she wards off potential nest raiders—chiefly bluegills—that the smaller male would otherwise have to spend energy chasing away. She maintains her vigil for up to 3 days of the 5-day hatching process—a period during which the male stockpiles energy for his solo defense of the eggs—and often makes the critical difference in egg survival. Because of her aggressive posture, the female is more vulnerable to being caught during this critical period than at any other time of the year.

Throw Whatever's Weird

Notoriously selective feeders, lunker bass usually strike only live bait or extremely realistic lures retrieved with a true-to-life action. But when their defensive instincts take over during spawning season and they're forced to stay put on the nest, they strike at anything they suspect is alive. Although I have never heard it said, it must be true that bass approach a lure as optimists. Otherwise, they could simply reject it from afar, without taking unnecessary risks and wasting precious energy. Your priority as an angler is simply to get your lure noticed and hope the bass ignores its unnatural aspects.

As a result, lurid colors—like bubble gum, chartreuse or even some-

*I*T'S ESTIMATED THAT THE EGGS OF ONLY 1 OUT OF 11 LARGEMOUTH NESTS SURVIVE PREDATION TO HATCH. Consequently, some people say that taking bass off the nest has negligible consequences. *Not true.* Spawn fishing targets large adult fish that can take years to replace. Keep these tips in mind:

▲ RELEASE FISH QUICKLY. If they're returned to the waters near their nest within 3 to 5 minutes of their capture, largemouths will resume spawning.

▲ "IF THE SHALLOWS ARE A ROCKIN' ...." Don't fish every active nest you see; leave some fish to complete the act of breeding without your interference.

▲ BECAUSE WATER TEMPERATURE, the main determinant of spawn timing, varies by several degrees from one end of a lake to the other, it's possible to avoid active nests in favor of pre- and post-spawn fish.

thing fluorescent—can be deadly during the late spawn. Even lures that represent creatures not native to the lake can be effective. Switch from worms to lizards; use gitzits, creepy crawlers, craw worms or big spinners and buzzbaits.

In the animal world, red is the color that challenges—and that goes for a Georgia farm pond as well as a Barcelona bullring. For largemouths, the relevance of red comes from the high iodine count in their eggs, which lends a scarlet hue to egg-eating minnows. Bass have evolved a high degree of sensitivity to this color over the millennia. So if there's one thing all of your spawn lures should have in common, it's a splash of red.

Which is appropriate considering the spawn is a time of war for largemouths. Anything alive is the enemy, and even the largest females are not going to stop to ask for ID papers before they strike. This is your brief view into their combative, captivating world. This is your magic time, too.

Some Like It Hot

by Doug Hannon

As summer sets in, water temperature determines exactly where largemouths prowl.

———————

WORLD-RECORD LARGEMOUTH bass: 22 lb. 4 oz., caught by George Perry, Montgomery Lake, Georgia, June 2, 1932. Perhaps the single most significant fact about bass fishing is expressed at the end of that statement— that the year's peak feeding activity occurs from late spring to mid-summer, when the water temperature is within that magic window of 70° to 85°F.

The warmth fuels cold-blooded metabolisms to such a frenzy that fish possess the appetite of garbage disposals and the disposition of chain saws. And that, as George Perry proved, includes the biggest largemouths.

Many bass anglers catch their largest fish during spring, and subsequently harbor the mistaken belief that the presence of eggs in large females makes fish heavier during breeding than at any other time of year. In truth, it is fat, not roe, that has the greatest potential of adding girth to a bass by far.

Consider a normal 10-pound bass, which typically has a length of about 26 inches and a girth of 17. At most, that fish—or indeed a breeding bass of any size—might carry a single pound of eggs. If that extra pound of weight sounds substantial, imagine the super-fat, 26-inch-long fish that have come out of the fabled Southern California reservoirs, 17-, 18-, and even 20-pound bass that tape up to *28 inches around*, carrying close to *10 pounds of fat*. Mark my words: Fat is where it's at, and when the next world-record bass hits the scales, her weight will probably be comprised of close to 50 percent fat and no more than 5 percent eggs.

The scientific truth is, bass feed and grow more during the warm months than at any other time of the year, which is why summer, not spring, is "the best of all bass seasons."

The Summer Migration

In terms of finding peak-season bass habitat, I want you to put all that pro-babble about "structure" and "patterning" aside and revert to a more natural sense of perception and terminology. Since we're talking about feeding fish, our main considerations should be finding an abundance of prey in the type of habitat that can be easily exploited by hungry bass. Largemouths are best suited for hunting in relatively shallow water (less than 20 feet) and are most successful when using ambush tactics. They appear out of nowhere and, using a burst of acceleration along with their superb maneuverability, overtake and instantly engulf their quarry along with half a gallon of water flushed through their gills. Bass do not do well in the long chase, so cover is a key to successful hunting.

Baitfish, over any other prey (frogs, bugs, etc.), are usually the only food source that exists in the abundance—and with the vulnerability—necessary to sustain bass through this intense 70° to 85°F feeding period. The most likely place to find bait is on flats with a large quantity and variety of cover. (I would define "flats" as large expanses of gradually sloping bottom over which the depth increases 5 feet or less for every 100 yards you proceed toward deep water.) The best flats progress out to depths of 20 feet or so, over a distance ranging from several hundred yards to more than a mile, and then exhibit a quick drop into a channel or the deepest water in a lake. As a general rule, water temperature influences the specific position of fish on the flats. As bass move out of the coves and bays where they spawn, they filter onto the shallow side edges of flats. As the season pro-

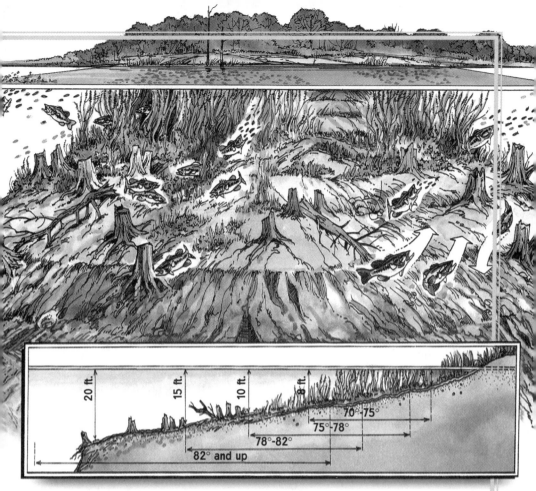

WARMING TRENDS: After spawning, bass gravitate to large concentrations of vulnerable prey, most frequently flats-roaming baitfish. The very best flats are extensive and gradually sloping, dropping no more than 5 feet per 100 yards and extending more than a ¼ mile out from shore before falling off sharply into a lake's deepest water. As the water warms through the 70s and into the 80s, it pushes bass from weedy cover in the shallows to woody cover in deeper water; eventually they lurk near severe drop-offs, where they can make brief forays back onto the flat and hit baitfish schools streaming in from open water.

gresses, rising temperatures drive the fish's metabolisms—hence, food requirements—to increased levels, and the bass move farther up onto the flat in search of the most abundant baitfish in the thickest concentrations.

Once temperatures reach the bass's metabolic peak, the fish gravitate to the steepest edges in order to maintain the closest contact with their food source up on the flats, while still having access to cooler water. When temperatures start to drop in the fall, the bass again move up onto the flat proper, before making their final annual move down those same steep slopes into deep winter quarters. The pattern applies to submerged humps as well. The only difference is that the scenario starts when the water reaches 75°F, since the most productive humps tend to top out about 8 feet below the surface, and there are no extreme shallows for fish to connect with.

Perhaps the best news about the post-spawn feeding migration is that the larger female bass complete their role as spawners before the eggs hatch, while the smaller males are left back in the nursery for several weeks to protect the fry. This means that the first occupants of these summering flats are predominantly big female bass, and the same migration pattern often is true about a month later when the fish move onto submerged open-water humps.

Lure Selection Simplified

In the first stage of the season (70° to 75°F), bass are making their initial adjustments to moving onto the flats. They do not yet know what specific species of prey they will encounter and have not yet become selective in feeding on the most common baitfish in the area. As a result you can afford to be versatile in your selection of lures, so long as you choose flashy, attention-getting items that opportunistic bass will interpret simply as "food." Of course, soft plastics like worms and tube lures are always worth a try, but this is one of the best times of the year for spinnerbaits, buzzbaits and noisy topwater lures fished aggressively. However, the one card that should not be left unturned is the plastic lizard. For some reason, these four-legged critters tend to outproduce plastic worms on early season bass by at least two to one. Good colors to start with are green, blue and black.

During the second stage (75° to 78°F), fish are at their most aggressive and can be caught from top to bottom in the water column. While soft plastics and bottom-contact lures can produce well at any time during this period, it's the best of times for topwaters, floater/diver minnows, Slug-Go-style soft jerkbaits and, especially, any number of unweighted swimming-worm rigs. The important thing is to emphasize lures that can be worked rather quickly, making it easy to cover all areas of the water column between the bottom and the surface. Bass in the 3- to 10-foot-depth range see your offerings as prey that's been caught out in the open, with no place to hide. It's a time of hard-charging strikes that can provide some of the most brawling action of the year.

The third stage (78° to 82°F) slows things down a bit and shifts activity a little deeper. There will still be plenty of shallow-water action, but keeping up with the big fish will require a change in strategy. Remember that in deeper water, 6 to 15 feet, weeds and cover will be somewhat harder to locate. One of the best things you can do is switch to contact baits and let your lures "feel" for bass-holding structure.

Jigs, plastic worms and Carolina-rigging all manner of soft plastics will produce. When active fish are found, however, it's hard to beat a slow-rolled spinnerbait or a big-lipped, super-buoyant crankbait with a 12- to 20-foot depth rating.

This brings us to the fourth and final stage of the peak season (82°F and up), when fish start dropping off the edges of flats and humps. The higher the temperature, the greater the metabolic demand for oxygen—but the less oxygen the water can hold. In reservoirs and flowing lakes this brings bass to the edges closest to the main current or other moving water. Weeds are scarce in the deeper water; consequently, the fish tend to hold on stumps, branches and other structure. Forage leans toward shad and other open-water baitfish. So in addition to scouring the bottom with lead and soft plastics, you might add some silver to your routine in the form of jigging spoons, tail-spinners and grubs.

Remember, "flats" and "humps" might sound like contradictory terms, but if you are aware of the four stages and are willing to stay in touch with the fish, they could be your key to the best of all bass seasons.

Bass in a Flood

by Jerry Gibbs

High water doesn't mean you have to take a rain check on fishing.

THE FLOOD CAN COME AT ANY time in any season. It can paint the water the color of cigar wrapper, make lakes flow like rivers, create new structure, destroy old, chill the water or warm it. The flood can be good, or can be bad. *When* it comes, and *how much* of it comes, determines what it will do to the bass fishing . . . and how you'll need to deal with it.

Winter rains do good things to river-run lakes. Because the rain will be relatively warmer than winter lake water, it perks up fish that were lolling around. Spring floods are different. Water that's already in the 50s gets no quick boost from a sudden deluge—unless it's been an unusually cool spring. Then, a soft rain followed by warming temperatures can do wonders, even if it does raise the water level.

Late-spring and summer storms also create or magnify lake currents. Dam masters in charge of release schedules can do the same thing. And wind can heighten the effect. If a substantial current is created, bass—especially largemouths—will eventually reposition into protected areas and slack water. The fish won't go as shallow as they do during extremely muddy conditions—look for them just out of the flow in places where the current is deflected and inside the mouths of tributaries, bays and coves.

When mud or heavy rains produce low-visibility water, forget silvery, reflective lures that rely on light. Go with either dark colors (such as black, brown or purple with a little red or white) or their total opposites (fluorescents, particularly in white, orange or chartreuse).

WHEN A CLEAR LAKE TURNS MUDDY, adopt a three-step approach:

1. FISH THE EDGE OF THE PLUME, also known as the "mud line."

2. IF THAT FAILS, look for pockets of clear water. You'll often find such waters trapped in coves, cuts and bays.

3. WHEN EVEN THESE CLEAR SPOTS ARE MISSING, fish the shallowest cover available. Flip worms, jigs with pork or plastic and spinnerbaits into brush, willows and stick-ups. Likewise, fish near banks using large lures that cause plenty of disturbance in the low-viz water. One final thought: If you know fish were holding deep—say 20 to 25 feet on offshore structure—before muddy water hit, they should still be there. Mud is a surface-oriented phenomenon, leaving deep-holding fish relatively undisturbed.

Wash Out

High water presents a fishing challenge; an over-the-banks flood can be a genuine predicament. When sustained torrents pound a lake during a late, unseasonably cool spring, the fishing is almost always bad. Cold and incessant rains—even if there's no influx of mud—is one of the toughest fishing situations imaginable. Add a dose of snow runoff, and it *is* the toughest situation.

Eddie La France and I had it like that recently on a natural northern lake. The water was *10 feet* over norm, maybe more, and it had been even higher. Launching ramps were out of commission, shorelines were submerged, homes were flooded, and you could run a boat where farmers should have been running their John Deeres. When the week-long rains finally quit, the tail of the front kissed us good-bye with wind and that other wonder of high pressure—cold air.

If there's a rule of thumb about finding largemouths that will hit in high water, especially the chocolate-colored water we were facing, it's to get away from main channels, get shallow and get tight as a tick to cover. Largemouths have no love for heavy current. They want quiet water, and in muddy, high-water conditions, they'll pack up and move into the back ends of creeks and bays—even into canals—to find it.

The bass we were dealing with began making their moves during the few warm days before the bad weather came again. They were fleeing a flooded bay filled with strong currents by running up a dead-end creek. We caught them by twitching floating Rapalas on the down-current side of a giant culvert through which the fish had to travel to cut themselves some slack. Tractor-trailers shrieked by a few feet behind us—not exactly postcard fishing. Then the water came again, and the chill. Eventually, the culvert flooded out.

Eddie and I then fished protected places *way* back in shallow, bushy cover. I poled the boat over a marsh where land critters normally walked. Mini-twisters blew. In one spot we used our electric motor to work a submerged tributary back through the flooded forest. We saw no forage, caught no fish. Under normal spring conditions, when bass begin moving shallow to spawn, cold fronts push them back to staging areas. Operating on that theory, we fished the deeper breaks near the only green vegetation around. Still nothing. There was only one option left, a sort of transition area between the deep and flooded shallows. But how should we pinpoint it?

The few fish we finally scratched out came under a very specific set of conditions. There was a flooded point extending into deeper water. Small willows that were now standing in water grew along the point. Where the willows gave way to rocky rubble, Eddie took a nice smallie. I tagged a largemouth near the hidden outflow of a major tributary, lying tight to an angled log sticking from the water. Another smallie ate at a flooded point extending off an island. All these spots had one thing in common: The water was so calm as to be slick, but it lay close to water being hit by wind, and near a drop-off to deeper water. That was the *only* pattern to produce for us, and to this day it's my natural-disaster routine.

Back to School

by Doug Hannon

For late-season largemouths,
smart anglers study the baitfish.

MOST ANGERS ARE WELL-VERSED in how to fish the bass spawn, but ask them about late-season largemouth behavior and they'll act like you've asked for the atomic number of strontium. That's because every outdoors magazine worth the paper it's printed on publishes big feature articles on the spawn every year, while the movements and patterns of bass during late summer and fall get very little coverage. As a result of this knowledge gap, uninformed and confused anglers spend the end of the season motoring aimlessly around their favorite lakes looking for fish.

SQUEEZE PLAY: Locating tight schools of baitfish in open water can be time-consuming and frustrating. But you can beat the odds by focusing on areas where baitfish are *forced* to concentrate, such as bottlenecks between areas of open water (right) or humps that compress the water column (below). Find a spot that has both, and you may end up in the middle of a bass feeding frenzy.

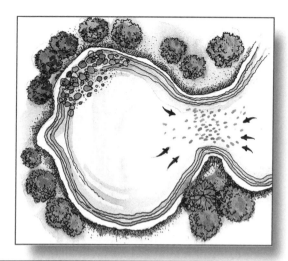

Part of the problem is that scientists seem to be interested only in sex, focusing their microscopes on largemouth reproductive cycles. Attempts to establish a clear understanding of the late-season habits of bass are left to the "unscientific" analysis of generations of opinionated, gunwale-side naturalists. But the situation isn't hopeless—every backlash can be turned into a full spool of castable line, *if* you are patient and willing to sort out all the knots and tangles. If over the course of a season I've learned only one or two truths about the nature of bass, or of fishing, that can be relied on, I consider that a good year. My success as a bass angler has come from realizing how few things are known for sure and from learning to rely on those high-leverage truths. With that in mind, let's take a look at some of the fundamental facts that are the keys to successful late-season bass fishing: *How the fish and its forage relate to weather and other environmental factors.*

By fall, all the prey and forage species in a lake have reproduced and grown to their maximum size. Because the food chain is peaking in both abundance and variety of forage—and because their reproductive duties are long behind them—bass assume the role of pure predators, with nothing on their minds but food. They focus their activity *away* from the banks at this time of year, as opposed to the early season when they direct their energies toward shorelines and shallow flats and into coves or pockets.

More than ever, then, the name of the game for late-season fishermen is to locate the baitfish, because that's invariably where you'll find the bass. The problem is that, because ever-changing weather extremes keep the bait—and, consequently, the bass—constantly on the move, the bass are here today and gone tomorrow. These weather-driven bait migrations, more than all other factors, account for the rapid changes in fishing action that anglers experience in late summer and fall. One day the fish are concentrated and easy to catch; the next they're scattered and extremely tough to pattern. One of the best late-season strategies, therefore, is to learn the weaknesses of a *particular type of baitfish* and to be there when the bass exploit it.

Having had all summer to grow, bite-size shad are now a top-priority food source—tasty morsels for largemouths of all sizes. But bass are most comfortable and best adapted to hunting from structure, whereas shad are known to be an open-water (pelagic) baitfish. So it takes a tremendous concentration of bait in tight quarters to generate a productive feeding scenario for bass. If you can pinpoint the spot where this concentration of bait occurs, you might be rewarded with giant schools of "eat anything" largemouths literally shredding surfacing pods of panicked shad.

How do you find these hotspots? Most anglers rely on the old standbys—looking for diving birds, for example. But an even better tool is an understanding of the lifestyle of the shad, knowledge that can help you to be there waiting when pandemonium erupts on the surface.

Shad travel in large, dense schools. Swimming with their mouths agape, they feed on plankton and algae suspended throughout the water column. They combat predators by grouping up into a tight mass that looks like a huge, solid ball of bait. This confuses predator fish because it offers them no individual target to strike at. Unlike most fish, therefore, shad avoid structure and cover which force the school to break up, making this "balling defense" impossible.

To feed on shad, bass are forced to abandon structure and employ

FISHING THE FALL SPAWN

ANOTHER LATE-SEASON ODDITY IS THE "FALL SPAWN." In many southern waters, as the temperature drops through 70°F and into the 60s—and especially if the water stays between 70° and 65°F for 2 to 3 weeks—male bass start fanning nests, females come in and lay eggs and a full spawn, complete with hatch, occurs. This phenomenon most commonly takes place in flowing water, but many of the famous Florida lakes, such as Okeechobee, have a fall spawn every year. Because such waters usually enjoy mild winters, the eggs hatch and the young can survive with plenty to eat. If the young do make it, they pass on the genes for fall spawning to future generations, and the cycle continues.

If you find yourself fishing the fall spawn, don't worry about late-season tactics. Simply adapt the advice you've gleaned from the myriad articles on fishing the spring spawn, and you're in business.

tactics that generally would be considered foreign to their nature. So look for places where shad will be concentrated not too far from cover. Any kind of bottleneck, which tends to compress and concentrate schools of baitfish as they pass through, makes the shad much more vulnerable to attack. (The ideal situations are illustrated on page 75.) The narrow throat or bottleneck connecting one area of open water to another can create a two-way compression effect on schools of bait passing through. Schools that are evenly distributed throughout the water column are concentrated as they pass through the narrows between points.

The situation becomes even more attractive to bass if the water in the narrows is shallow, creating a two-dimensional squeeze, thereby doubling the effect. Bass will hang on the downwind side of the lip, using the slope of the hump to drive their quarry toward the surface, where the bass can cut the school to pieces. Even if the two points coming together consist of weeds, brush or timber, that can be enough to funnel schools of shad and create likely bass-schooling areas as well. Lipless crankbaits, minnow imitations (from topwater

CIRCLING GULLS often pinpoint the location of largemouths feeding on shad.

to mid-depth lures) and even silver spoons can be deadly. Since the bass usually "work" the bait in brief spurts, I use a single-hooked lure, because it's quicker to unhook the fish and get back in action. Among my favorites are a white bucktail jig or a soft-plastic swimming grub in smoke, smoke with silver glitter or pearl colors.

As the season progresses and water temperatures drop into the low 50s, the dreaded and misunderstood "fall turnover" occurs. With each passing day, cold fronts increase in frequency and severity, chilling the surface of the lake. When water cools, it becomes more dense, causing it to sink. The deep, warmer water underneath then rises to the top—hence "turnover." The water rising to the top can be turbid, low in dissolved oxygen and even foul-smelling—which can slam the door on productive fishing, often for several weeks. Most fishermen

simply park the boat, put the rods in the garage and watch football until the water temperatures balance out. But, as with any large-scale adversity, there are a few windows of opportunity left open for crafty anglers.

Principal among these windows are those parts of a lake where there is well-oxygenated water near the surface; these become havens for baitfish and bass. And this is the one period of the late season when bass abandon their open-water haunts and *do* focus on the edges of lakes. One such widely overlooked place is the extreme shallows on windswept shorelines. Wave action oxygenates the water and then the wind concentrates it against the shoreline. Bass can sometimes be found pushing bait so far up on the bank that their backs part the water. Use minnow-imitating twitchbaits like Rapalas and A.C. Shiners where the waves lap the shoreline, and you can make "turnover" work to your advantage.

Another productive tactic is to locate creeks with clean, oxygenated water coming into the lake. The baitfish sometimes flood up these streams in such densities that it is commonly called a "false spawn." Often there is so much bait that the bass are as stuffed as Uncle Tubby after the pig roast and holding in structure such as trees, brush or weeds along the banks. Look for baitfish activity on the surface; the bass won't be far. Impulse lures like spinner-baits or a jig 'n pig fished in or close to cover can be productive, but when the fish get active, a buzzbait is hard to beat.

My best advice to those lucky enough to be on the water during the late season is to fish as often as you can, and keep your hopes high. But leave your ego at home, or you're bound to bruise it on those days when you can't buy a bite. If you give yourself enough chances, you're sure to enjoy some banner days along with the inevitable skunkings. And when someone tries to tell you that this is the season when fishing is a sure thing, don't fall for it.

Don't Let the Game Go Cold

by Rich Zaleski

*When winter cools down the action,
you can better your chances.*

THE ODDS SEEM STACKED AGAINST the winter bass angler. His cold-blooded quarry's metabolism is at its annual low point, so he's after fish that are prone to move neither far nor fast to snag a meal. And when a bass does work up the energy to eat something, biologists tell us it digests so slowly that it might not need to feed again for days or even weeks. Then there's the likelihood of prolonged periods of "lockjaw" due to severe temperature changes. Given all these negatives, it's easy to conclude that cold-water bass fishing is a losing proposition.

COLD-WATER NIRVANA: Deep water, a steep rocky bluff, a nearby creek confluence . . . and not another angling soul in sight.

Deep Thoughts

THE AUTHOR with a fall smallie taken on a jig.

It can be just that, if you apply rest-of-the-season mentality to your winter bass fishing. However, for anglers who understand the unique keys to frigid-water bass success, it's anything but. Those keys are stress, environmental stability, aggregation . . . and a good supply of jigs.

It's too soon to talk lures, however. The first three factors are so important that more than any other time of year, it's imperative that we find the fish before we worry about what will catch them.

Rapid changes in water conditions are always stressful for bass, but in cold water, their bodies adjust more slowly and the trauma lasts longer. In an attempt to avoid such stress, bass hole up in areas that are insulated from, or at least mitigate, fluctuations in the weather. Usually (but not always) that means deep water. Other locations that provide environmental stability are submerged springs, warm-water discharges from power plants and off-current backwaters in rivers.

Bass in Bunches

Location is the paramount concern in winter bass fishing, because when large numbers of fish move into limited areas, it only figures that the rest of the lake can be nearly devoid of fish. While a few "strays" may make the day interesting, don't be lulled: The first concern is identifying the kinds of places bass are likely to bunch.

Thirty-some-odd winters of experimenting have provided me with guidelines to finding the deep spots that hold bass in the winter. If there's current in the body of water you are fishing, seek out the deepest spot *without* current, or at least with the slowest current. Look for the sharpest drop-offs and steepest breaking shorelines. Within reason, find the deepest hard bottom in the lake, and key on bulky cover. For example: Stumps on a rocky bottom are better than brush on a muddy bottom. If a creek channel intersection can be included into the terrain mix, the probability is very good that you'll encounter bunched-up bass.

Reduced activity levels and slow digestion aside, when the fish are crowded into small areas, chances for success rise. Few fish might be willing to bite at any given moment, but when your lure almost bumps noses with dozens of them on each cast, the sheer numbers say that the odds get friendlier. Not just because you have a better chance of finding a hungry fish, but because the natural competitiveness for food becomes a factor in your favor.

Just Jigs

Offer those crowded fish something that looks natural, and the odds get better yet. In this case, "looking natural" means moving your lure as if it were as lethargic as the bass themselves—and not displaying any traits that might inhibit or alarm a bass. In short, it means a jig. Sure, there are winter days when you can catch bass on a deep-diving crankbait or a spinnerbait, but a jig of one type or another will usually work then too. And a jig will also work on the far more numerous winter days when nothing else in your box will.

The knowledgeable winter specialist's tackle box is loaded with jigs, jigheads and jigging spoons. They will range from full-sized "bass

DRESS IN LAYERS, wear a warm hat, and cold air temps won't keep you from experiencing some of the hottest fishing of the entire season.

jigs" to ⅛-ounce hair or marabou jigs that look more like they were intended for crappies. In between, you'll find an assortment of lead-heads and flat or "boot-tail" plastic grubs. Swimming-tail grubs? Be cautious in using these. They'll work in cold weather, but much of the time the winter bass angler doesn't move his lure fast enough to make a swimming-tail swim.

The most productive colors blend with the environment—black, brown, smoke, watermelon and the like. Remember, you're trying to make a jig look and act like natural prey that is trying not to be noticed as it makes its way through an area full of bass. Marty Wencek, a fine winter angler with a background in fishery biology, offers some insight into how bass locate prey (or lures) in the 15- to 40-foot depths at which we usually find them in cold water.

"Even in moderately clear water, a fish can't see much more than a silhouette at those depths," he says. "But everything that moves through the water creates 'displacement waves,' and a bass senses that motion through the lateral line running down its side. Especially with fish grouped tightly like they usually are in winter, one of them is bound to notice it before long. If they're not finding your lure, it's probably because you're not fishing where they are. If you suspect they're finding it but not biting, then go to a more natural color. They're likely to be turned off by bright, unnatural colors."

Once you've mastered the keys, the odds against winter bass success don't seem so bad after all. In fact, when you conjure up an image of your lure surrounded by a gang of fish in their deep lair, it's easy to conclude that coldwater bass fishing can be an "easy pickings" proposition.

Undercover Secrets

by Doug Hannon

It's no mystery that largemouths use shadowy cover to ambush their prey, but exactly how these fish hunt may surprise you.

HEAVY COVER IS BOTH THE HAVEN and the hunting ground of largemouth bass. So inextricably linked are bass and weeds that it seems the fish evolved specifically to play its predatory role amid the weed-walled galleries beneath the surface of lakes and rivers. But the correlation wasn't always so apparent.

Several decades ago, most bass fishermen looked for the major structural element of a lake and fished its edges. Funny how this expansive field of fire has become tight aquatic jungle warfare. Where perhaps 75 percent of all bass fishing occurred in open water with treble-hooked lures, now most of it requires snag-proof rigs inched through swamps-in-training. Get on a new bass lake and where do you go? The weeds of course. Show me hydrilla! Lily pads! Deadfalls! The more, the better.

Although this bass-weed connection is universally acknowledged, precious few fishermen understand *how* bass use cover. We've all read things like bass can be found in extremely shallow structure at times when the best fishing is thought to be in deep water; or pros always seem to be able to catch fish by flipping and pitching in thick stuff; or fallen trees seem to hold more fish than standing timber; or overhead cover in the shallows is often productive even during the brightest periods; or a change in lure color can sometimes save the day.

As we read these statements we accept each as an independent truth, when, in fact, a common thread connects them all . . . and others. Seeing that thread—what we'll call the "rest of the story"—will make us better anglers.

So, with apologies to Paul Harvey, here's Page Two as it relates to bass and cover.

Truth:

Bass hold tight to cover in cloudy or turbid water.

Rest of the Story:

When it comes to bass fishing, I can think of nothing more important than this: Bass are primarily sight feeders. Unfortunately, most of us remember the exceptions to the rule better than the rule itself. Among those too-vivid exceptions: that bass can be caught on dark, moonless nights; that bass strike bright lures out of aggression; that they home in on certain tastes; that they're attracted to rattling and clicking and whirring.

Put these exceptions aside. Concentrate on the fact that bass are sight feeders. And because they're sight feeders, we need to understand how light behaves down there.

Under normal circumstances, water is relatively turbid, with a visibility of no more than 3 or 4 feet. Like us, bass need visual clues to find their way around a stump to point the way to a weed mat just through that haze off on the right, and so on. If a bass is using cover to hide in and hunt from, that cover ceases to exist when the fish wanders away from it into the featureless soup all around. For this, and no other reason, the mystery of why bass tend to stay very tight to cover in cloudy and dark water is solved. They don't want to get lost. End of story.

That also explains why, under those same turbid conditions, fishing tends to be most productive in shallow water—the visibility is better there. Whether you're fishing in deep or shallow water, however, always fish near the surface in cloudy water. Fish can see your lure from farther away. Moreover, when a shallow-running lure is backlit by the sun bass can see it better than if it just swims past them horizontally. Simply getting your lure noticed is the job here. Go gaudy and gradual: Fish big, bright, shallow-running lures slowly.

Truth:

A change in lure color can sometimes save the day.

Rest of the Story:

Two new words everyone should have in their fishing vocabulary are "reflection" and "refraction." Whenever light passes from one medium to another—say from air to water—it meets resistance. Some light fails to enter that second medium and instead bounces off the interface. The greater the angle of

Fig. 1: Reflection

incidence—that is, the lower the angle of approach—the greater the resistance.

That explains why glare on a lake's surface (reflected light) is most evident when the sun sits low in the sky. If the principle

of reflection is obvious when light travels through the air and hits a lake's surface, it is even more pronounced under water, when light passes from the water back into the air. Anyone who has ever skin-dived knows that to see up through the surface you practically have to roll over on your back. Even then, there's only a small, round viewing window; the rest of the surface has turned into a mirror. With this mirror-effect in mind, realize that when the water is relatively clear and shallow, the surface reflects the *bottom*.

Bass sometimes use surface reflection as a predatory ploy. It enables them to hide completely out of sight, buried in a mat of weeds or behind a fallen tree, while using the overhead surface mirror to get an aerial view of approaching baitfish (see Fig. 1, p. 87). Because these bass are monitoring the bottom when they're really looking up (remember, it's a reflection), lures fished on or near the surface will be more visible to the fish if they contrast with the color of the bottom. Most fishermen take this into account when they're fishing near the bottom; very few do when they're fishing on or near the surface. In short, dark lures and flies—especially dark-*backed* lures—should be one of your first choices over a light bottom, and vice versa.

As an aside, the reflection principle can also be used to hide things— your boat, for instance. I always paint the sides of my aluminum boat in a camouflage pattern of green and blue, but leave the bottom unpainted so that the metallic silver finish blends in with the mirror-like surface of the water. In essence, the boat's bottom becomes virtually invisible by reflecting the natural colors below it.

Truth:

Pitching and flipping far back under thick lily pads can be extremely effective.

Rest of the Story:

As we pointed out in the previous section, some of the light traveling from air to water will be reflected. That's fairly straightforward stuff. Here comes the hard part: The portion of light that manages to enter the water does not proceed in straight lines. It bends, or "refracts."

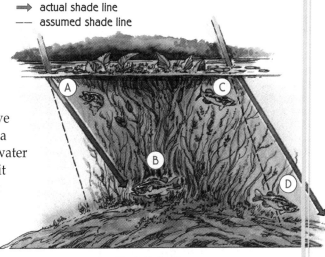

→ actual shade line
-- assumed shade line

Fig. 2: Refraction

An example: At one time or another, we've all pushed the tip of a fishing rod into the water and discovered that it appears to bend as it breaks through the surface. That "bent" fishing rod follows the path of light entering the water. Native Americans referred to this phenomenon as "the bending of the arrow" and used it with great skill to successfully aim slightly below underwater targets.

The principle of refraction is particularly applicable around surface cover. When a mat of lily pads is lit from the front, for example, its underwater shadow bends *under* the pads, making the shade line hit the lake bottom much farther under the cover than you might think (Fig. 2, above).

Generally, active bass hover near the water's surface, while inactive fish hold near the bottom. Applying refraction, then, active fish will hold near the top edge of front-lit surface cover [A], while inactive bass will hold near the bottom *much farther back* beneath the cover than one would assume [B].

In practical fishing terms, you should tackle the situation this way: First try those potentially active fish near the edge, then pitch in deeper. Use heavier lures in the thick stuff—the bigger the better. You'll need the weight to get the lure down and the size to get it noticed through the tangle of vegetation.

If the weed mat is backlit, the situation is reversed: You're likely to find active fish right on the edge of the cover again [C], but you might also encounter inactive fish on the deeper shade line well *away* from the vegetation canopy [D].

Truth:

Overhead cover in the shallows is often productive even during the brightest periods of the day.

Rest of the Story:

As a photographer, I know that, on average, there's four times as much light in direct sun than there is in the shade (the exposure correction is two f-stops). The same ratio applies between open water and deeply shaded cover.

Because underwater light diminishes with increasing depth and with shade, I sought to derive a reasonable aquatic equivalent to the rule. It's what I call "Hannon's overhead cover factor": If you find fish active at a particular depth in open water, you can expect to find them in heavy cover at one-fourth that depth. Think of it this way: Whenever you see a stand of thick weeds or even a dock in the open shallows, consider it a deep hole. And anybody who would pass up a 16-foot hole in 4-foot shallows would be crazy.

Truth:

Fallen trees seem to hold more fish than standing timber.

Rest of the Story:

As a final note, let me reiterate that shade is the reason bass hold close to cover—shade to hide in and shade to hunt from. Since bass do not like to waste energy moving, and just a little shade is all they need, the presence of *constant* shade often determines whether bass will or won't use a particular form of cover.

Nowhere is this more apparent than with trees. A leaning or fallen tree always hold more, and bigger, bass than a standing tree. The reason: When the sun is overhead, a standing tree casts little or no shadow, but there is no sun angle or time of day when a tree lying horizontal will not offer some shade.

So when you're dealing with bass in cover, remember this: The rules haven't changed, just the reasons for following them.

. . . And now you know the *rest* of the story.

Floating for Bronzebacks

by Michael Hanback

*For early summer fun, you can't beat a
float-trip for smallmouths.*

I LIKE TO SHOVE OFF IN THE LOW-
angle light of dawn. As the current
sweeps my canoe around the first
bend of the mist enshrouded stream,
wood ducks often flush, squealing, from

beneath an oak tree. An otter might swim within paddle's reach. Sometimes a doe and her fawns, red and beautiful in summer coats, mill about on a sandbar. I've floated this stretch hundreds of times, but I always smile when I do. This little river is still as wild as they come. It's a place where I can hook anywhere from 50 to 100 scrappy smallmouth bass on a good day of fishing.

Anatomy of a Smallmouth Stream

In river environments, the smallmouth, or bronzeback, is a "tween-er." Check topographical maps and aerial photographs for winding, moderate-gradient stretches that lie below cold, mountain-born trout creeks but above warm, lazy largemouth rivers. Typically, these middle waters are streams that average only 2 to 6 feet deep in summer. You can skip a flat rock across them in many places. But with a nice mix of current, cover and food, these are the waterways that offer prime smallmouth habitat.

In canoeist's language, a good smallmouth stream has Class 1, 2 or 3 rapids every half-mile or so. These gentle to moderately swift riffles keep the water clear, cool and oxygenated. Emerald-enshrouded pools and eddies swirl above and below the white water. Here bronzebacks hold like brown trout, sucking in insects and larvae that tumble by and probing the rocky bottoms for minnows, crayfish and hellgrammites.

Between the riffles curl stretches of smooth, slower-moving water canopied by trees and strewn with rocks, logjams and cut banks. Here, bronzebacks live up to their old Indian name *achigan* ("ferocious"), darting out from beneath shadowy structure to attack the odd minnow or snatch terrestrial insects fluttering on the surface.

Float-Fishing Strategies

June through October is the time to launch a canoe and pan for bronze. Rivers and streams in smallmouth country are shallow and clear now, with water temperatures between 65° and 80°F—perfect for bass activity. Fish that were scattered in the spring are settled into summer patterns that will hold until mid-autumn. Gregarious yet territorial, bronzebacks school in cool, shady habitats and hammer baits on or near the surface.

Pools and eddies above and below riffles are especially good places to fish. Paddle your canoe close, and cast lures up and across the current. Work spinners or crankbaits fairly fast to keep them wobbling

RIVER SMALLIES are not only willing biters, they're acrobatic fighters.

realistically. I like to drift plastic grubs and worms through pools and eddies. The current grabs the supple lures and pulls them down into the shady, rocky crevices where big bass hang out.

A strip of rippling water hard against a shoreline is always a good place to look for bass. The water may be only a foot or two deep, but that's all a smallmouth needs. Colored so as to be perfectly camouflaged amid the mottled shadows and gravelly bottom, they'll fin confidently, nabbing minnows and swarming insects that fall from bankside foliage and tree limbs. Paddle quietly toward cut banks, then zip plugs, worms or plastic jerkbaits deep into the shade.

If a fish hits, drop anchor and keep casting. Sometimes 4, 6, maybe even 10 smallies of similar size will school in such lies. When one fish smashes a lure, the others become more aggressive.

Many anglers think that stream smallmouths are strictly swift-water fish. In their zeal to get to the next rapid or riffle, these fishermen paddle past what they consider to be dead water—the deep, slow-moving, foam-flecked stretches. Big mistake. Those spots often produce plenty of fish, and big ones at that.

Maneuver your canoe within 30 yards of rocks or piles of driftwood in still water. Cast lures up and beyond the structure and retrieve them deep and slow. I catch my biggest bass by flipping plastic worms and bumping them back across bottom. In deep holes, bronzebacks, especially the largest ones, often hit a lure on the dead drift.

Another misconception is that bass are most active at dawn and dusk during the heat of summer. That's simply not the case. Smallmouths often go on feeding frenzies between noon and 4 p.m. If you're not fishing all day, you're missing out.

On a Virginia river last August, a buddy and I caught 30 smallmouths before lunch. Some were decent fish, 1- to 2½ -pounders, but that's still fairly poor action for us. Then, at 1 p.m., the sun burned through the clouds and broiled us, pushing the mercury into the 90s. Bass time!

We floated another 3 miles and hooked almost 75 more fish. With the take-out bridge in sight and the sun hotter than ever, I casted a Slug-Go into one last sliver of shade. A bomb went off as a big 4-pounder took me on a ride.

The bass bulldogged for bottom and just sat there. Finally he rose, and shot into the sky, olive sides glistening. Two leaps and three runs later the bronze beauty finned alongside the boat. I reached down, popped loose the hook and smiled as he finned away. Then I broke down my rods and paddled for the bridge, thinking, "Yeah, this little river is still as wild as they come."

Triggering
Strikes

Going with the Gold

by Jerry Gibbs

Every fish likes golden shiners—especially largemouth bass. In fact, golden shiners probably provide more big bass than any other bait.

THEY CAME SPILLING FROM THE cast net, glittering like nice small-stream trout in the morning sun. My guide grabbed them quickly, flipping them into the insulated, aerated cooler. I snatched one of the little fish and examined it carefully, thinking that I'd been mistaken and that the trophy bass man was not collecting the bait he said he needed but instead making a quick haul for dinner. Or maybe he would surprise me for lunch.

A TROPHY LARGEMOUTH will aggressively take a large goldern shiner suspended below a float.

"What are you going to do with these?" I asked.

"Fish with 'em," he said.

"How big are your bass?"

"You'll see," he said.

The trout-size minnows were 10 and 11 inches long. They were shiners. Golden ones. The smallest bass they caught that day weighed 7 pounds.

My introduction to big bass caught on this bait of equally impressive proportions occurred a long time ago. Since then, I've fished golden shiners in sizes ranging from a more realistic 3 inches right up to those big daddies, which are the ultimate weapon of trophy bass hunters. I wasn't off base about lunching on the critters, I learned.

Pan-size goldens support a sport fishery of their own, ending up dredged in cornmeal and skillet-fried by light-tackle enthusiasts in Southern climes where the species grows big enough.

Almost every fish likes golden shiners. Largemouths, stripers, white perch, smallmouths, pickerel, spotted and white bass, lake trout, and even walleyes will eat them gleefully in the proper sizes. It's bass, however, that concerns us here. Golden shiners probably provide more big bass than any other bait.

Goldens are sometimes called pond shiners or golden roaches (which they obviously are not, but somewhat resemble in profile). Their natural range is from Manitoba to Quebec, down through much of the eastern United States, and as far south as Mexico and Florida. Because of their productiveness as a bass bait, goldens have been legally and illegally introduced to many Western areas. In the 1970s, when hard-core California anglers were hot on the trail of the largemouth world record, a great deal of money was spent to air-freight goldens to the West Coast. In the South, they are by far the most widely used bait minnow. From Oklahoma to Ohio to Florida, dealers spend more time breeding and raising these shiners than other baits. One dealer in Arkansas sold more than one million pounds of goldens in a single year. What makes this fish so appealing to bass and other game species? A few things.

Nutritional excellence is one. It takes, on the average, 5 pounds of prey for a largemouth to gain 1 pound. A 14-inch bass would have to eat 60 6-inch gizzard shad or 80 4½-inch bluegills to gain that single pound. Only 45 7-inch golden shiners would give him the same weight gain. Other factors include profile and ease of consumption. Bass learn early that soft-rayed baitfish are a lot easier to handle than spiny-rayed critters such as bluegills and other small sunfish. Bass also quickly learn that elongated forage is easier to swallow than deep-bodied species. Maybe that's why they like plastic worms so. The golden shiner is even a little more streamlined in shape than a gizzard shad. Its lifestyle provides an additional reason to keep it right up front as major forage.

Golden shiners spawn in weedy areas of a lake, beginning at the end of their first year of life. Their sticky eggs adhere to rooted aquatic plants and also nonrooted algae. The shiners prefer clear lakes and quiet, clear pools in slow rivers. They are not very tolerant of silty water. Once they start spawning in the spring, they are likely to continue doing so right into the summer. This extended spawning means that there'll be a good supply of little golden shiners for juvenile largemouth or smallmouth bass to eat during the peak growing season.

The shiners are a schooling fish for all of their lives. They eat algae, plankton, insects (both adults and larvae) and tiny crustaceans. This should give you a clue as to their habitat—sometimes drowned brush, but always weeds. This is the same kind of habitat that shallow-oriented bass like. In other environments, however, bass may go most of their lives without seeing a golden. Offshore bass schools, for example, will likely do their main feeding on shad in many of the nation's reservoirs. Bass on riprap may be keyed on crayfish, and those in some Northern lakes could dine on a combination of emerald and other shiners as well as smelt when the latter forage species makes early and late-season movements near largemouth habitat.

Remember, however, that most populations of bass tend to move. Forage availability is one factor causing them to do so. If golden shiners occur in a given body of water, most bass will encounter them at some time during the year. And even if bass are oriented to cover or structure where other forage is prevalent, give them a chance at a golden and they will take it. They'll eat a golden shiner on the bottom, at mid-depth, or near the surface. Golden shiners stand out like the plumpest, ripest apple in the box; a single red pepper in a basket of green ones. Profile, soft fin rays, perhaps scent and, I feel, color act as triggering mechanisms that turn on the bass.

The color factor is one reason why many shiner fans like to catch their own. Straight from natural habitat, a healthy native golden shiner is yellowish on the belly though paler between the vent and pelvic fin, a section that has no scales (a good identification key). The lower sides are golden with silvery highlights, and the back and upper sides are golden-olive. When taken from tanks of bait retailers, many goldens seem to have changed color. Some blame it on chemicals used to reduce fungal and bacterial infections. Others think it's just the length of time that the bait stays in tanks. This is not to say that commercially raised shiners or wild ones trapped and held for sale are not good. They are. But when bass are particularly selective, the fresh-caught yellow-golden ones are just better.

When choosing goldens from a dealer, avoid those with red noses or traces of fungus. Also bypass those that are very dark or in the bottom corners of the tank because they are ready to die. Get your selection from those that are loosely schooled, the main group suspended in the tank. Another reason why shiner addicts like to catch their own is because it's usually the only way to have the biggest ones consistently on hand when you're hunting big bass.

How do you collect your own? There are a couple of good ways. Cast-netting is extremely effective. Choose an area where golden shiners naturally occur. Irregular places in weed beds, major bends in weed lines and small cove mouths are good. Consistent net-harvesting requires that you concentrate the shiners by chumming, or baiting, an area. Scatter chum in several spots the night before and just prior to netting. Wait a bit after scattering chum on netting day, then begin to harvest. A favorite chumming mix is a combination of oatmeal and chicken laying mash. A small net about 5 feet in diameter is easiest for beginners to handle.

A sweetened area also lends itself to angling for shiners. They'll take tiny spinners, plastic ice-fishing grubs, flies and bait such as dough-balls. You can use an ultralight spinning outfit, but a fly rod or a long cane pole and bobber can be most effective. The danger is that shiners demand a sensitive touch and critical timing when you strike. The game of angling for them can grow so intriguing that you forget your real purpose. You'll usually catch larger goldens by angling, but small and medium-size specimens are collected this way, too—especially when you're using doughballs and No. 12 hooks.

Golden shiners are most popular in the spring and to a lesser degree during the cooler-water period of the fall. Anglers are missing a good bet by not using them more during the summer. Sure, the bait is harder to keep alive in hot weather, but it's worth the effort. In the summer, goldens should be used on the day they're caught. Maximum life in a fishing situation is about 15 hours, often far less. Cool, well-oxygenated water is vital. Some anglers go to the extreme of attaching long plastic hoses to their bilge pump-type aerators and drawing water from the depths where they catch their shiners. That's good, but in torrid weather it won't keep the bait all day, even in an insulated bait tank.

You need to add ice or ice packs, not to chill the water, just to keep it from becoming too warm. Make sure that your ice is homemade, formed from non-chlorinated water.

In the summer, I like to use 3- to 6-inch-long shiners, the size I use for Northern-strain bass almost all of the time. With this size bait, I usually use No. 2/0 hooks. Summer bass can be more selective because of the abundance of natural forage. Their feeding—though heavy—may be for brief periods due to the readily available forage. A live golden shiner can often coax them to eat between feeding binges. It can also do some serious catching when hot-weather bass are on the feed. I stumbled upon that by accident.

I'd been shallow-fishing with goldens along a weed line one summer, having a slow go of it, when the water came alive some distance away. The action was not in the weeds, but offshore. The birds clued me in. I saw the gulls start to circle and then begin to dive, and I cranked in and hustled over there at full throttle, cutting down instantly when I saw fish breaking. I had on a fixed bobber set so that the bait was about 2 feet below the cork. I lobbed out my golden, and the first bass hit in seconds. It kept on going like that as long as the fish were up. They were feeding on shad. They weren't big bass—2½- to 3 pounds—but they made up for it in action and numbers. When the fish went down, I stayed.

When schooling bass sound, getting them to hit artificials can frequently be tough. I changed my rig to a slip-bobber setup so that I could hang my golden shiners at any depth I desired below the float. I found the bass about 12 feet down. I caught three more, and then the fishing cooled for a little bit. Then, the bass broke on the surface once again.

Since then, I've consistently taken bass by drifting or anchoring in an area where schooling bass have gone down. The technique is most effective if reefs, shoals, bars or humps are nearby. Make sure that your bobber is just big enough to hold up the bait. That way, it won't create unnatural resistance when a smaller bass grabs the shiner and tries to pull it under.

Depending on the season and what the bass are doing, golden shiners can be effectively fished several ways. They can be slow trolled behind a cigar-shape float that holds them at the desired depth. You can stillfish with them in shallow water using a fixed float, or as mentioned, quite deep beneath a slip-bobber. The shiners can be poke-poled under weeds, pocket-fished with a special hooking procedure, or bottom-fished by casting or trolling with a slip-sinker or bottom-walking rig.

Back in the early 1970s, trophy bass specialist John McClannahan perfected several float-rig systems for fishing big shiners in Florida. His methods work fine today, though we now have refined reels for handling baitfishing assignments and rods that increase hooking success. The essence of the float rigs is gearing float size to bait, and bait to bass. Second, your monofilament line should be marked with a waterproof felt-tip pen about 40 to 45 feet from the bait. Attempting to set the hook beyond this distance vastly reduces your hook-ups, especially on big bass.

We have a number of bent-shank hooks today, such as the Tru-Turn, which rotates when you strike to help embed the point.

The superior points available today also help. Back when John was doing his serious fishing, he favored an Eagle Claw Model 84 short-shank hook. He bent the eye and the first one-half inch of shank down at a 45° angle toward the point; he felt that this resulted in the hook really digging in on the set. I also had some good results then by using a saltwater tuna hook with a short shank.

Slow trolling golden shiners is done along weed lines, breaks, riprap, points, bars, shoals or any area you think is likely to hold fish. You use your electric motor (yes, oars and paddles still work) to creep along. The shiner is normally hooked either directly up through both lips or off-center up through the lower lip and out the nostril on the opposite side. Two small plastic disks or washers, or snips cut from a piece of surgical tube, are sometimes used as stops on the hook to prevent the hook from rehooking the bait rather than the bass when you strike. This is not such a problem when bent-shank hooks are used. A washer is slid over the point and up the bend; the shiner is then hooked and another washer slipped on. Washers are snugged next to the bait. Hook sizes are geared to your bait and fish, but normally run from a small No. 2/0 to a whopping No. 8/0. For trophy bass, especially near dense cover, few anglers will use lighter line than 25- or 30-pound-test when slow trolling or stillfishing. In open water, you can go down to 15- or 12-pound-test.

Cigar, bullet, or torpedo-shape floats troll better than round bobbers. There are a number of designs on the market that hold the float at a desired position on the line. You can also use a slip-float stopped between two barrel swivels, with a leader of desired length coming off the last swivel. If you want to troll with the bait at various depths, this is less handy.

Shiners are usually trolled 100 to 140 feet behind the boat, the rod placed into a holder. The approach of a bass will invariably cause your shiner to become frantic. Don't touch the rod until the bass takes the bait and begins running. Once that happens, all resistance on the line must be removed. Even the click of a revolving spool reel should be off, the outgoing line controlled by your thumb. Follow the fish as quietly as possible, keeping your shadow from crossing or falling on it. Your cat-and-mouse game has begun. The trick now is to get close enough. Before striking, you must bring in line until that magic 40 to 45-foot mark is at the tip guide. I've seen this game go on—line being gained and lost as the fish moved—for a timed 5 minutes! By then, all nerves were peaked beyond belief.

When the line mark comes in, raise your rod slowly, gently, until you feel the weight of the fish, then lower the tip, taking in line all the while to maintain contact with the bass. Then, hit it!

For stillfishing, a fixed rig is often used in shallow water. It uses a stopped bobber (use barrel swivels on either side of the float or the float's built-in stop) and 2 or 3 feet of leader. For deeper fishing, use a sliding float on the main line, then a barrel swivel, then a 2- to 3-foot leader. Add a few split shot 12 to 16 inches above the hook to get the bait down. On the main line, at any desired distance above the float, add a soft stop that can be reeled through the guides and onto your reel. You can use a bit of yarn, a sliding nail or a knot of Dacron or monofilament. There are also several sliding plastic stops that are available in tackle shops. Let the line slide through the bobber until it hits the soft stop, which may be 5, 10 or 20 feet up the line.

Stillfishing is done at all of the usual hotspots: man-made structure, weed beds, timber, and deep-water congregating spots, which you can also troll. Look for cuts and turns in the weed beds, especially if there is any change of depth associated with them. The shiners are usually hooked just aft of the dorsal fin for stillfishing. To head the bait where you want it to go, apply a little pressure with your rod, and it will try to swim in the opposite direction.

For pocket fishing in dense aquatic vegetation, try tail-hooking goldens. Try it with and without a little split shot 16 to 18 inches above the hook. The bait tends to swim down, and always away from pressure. You cannot do much retrieving with this method or you will drown the shiner.

In the South, thick beds of hyacinth are poke-poled using a 12- to 15-foot cane or fiberglass pole. A rubber band is slipped onto the end of the pole. Bait and a little line are stripped from your rod and reel outfit. The line is attached to the pole by tucking it up under the rubber band so that just 4 or 5 feet of it, plus bait, extends beyond the pole tip. Now, work along floating islands of hyacinth, milfoil beds or other vegetation, stalking with the careful quiet of a hunting heron, and stick the tip of the pole very gently beneath the weed

HEAVY-COVER SHINER RIGS consist of a 3-inch cylinder float and a special weedless shiner hook. Push the hook through the bottom of the shiner's jaw and out the nostril (inset). Set the weedguard and you're ready to fish.

mats. The bait moves back under there. When a bass eats it, the line snaps free of the rubber band, and you set the hook and fight the fish on your regular outfit. Be aware of sun shadows, and don't stick the long pole far under or wave it over an area where a fish is likely to lie.

For bottom fishing, the old slip-sinker rig is best when you want to cast and retrieve. Use a Lindy-Little Joe walking-sinker bait rig, or just a walking sinker with barrel-swivel stop plus any length leader on rocky bottoms. Use a plastic worm bullet-type slip sinker over brushy or weedy bottoms. Your leader should be 3 to 12 inches, depending how close you want to work the shiner to the bottom. For trolling along the bottom, use a rig such as the Gapen Bait Walker.

I like two-handed rods for fishing golden shiners. They should be no shorter than 7 to 7½ feet long. Trophy bass hunters often want tough 8½-foot salmon-type rods. Most big-bass hunters who use shiners want revolving-spool (casting) reels like the Abu Garcia Ambassadeur 6500C. Spinning was once considered out of the league by most who sought trophy bass with shiners. That changed with stronger construction and the introduction of dual drag systems, which allow a fish to take line past a closed bail against little or no resistance, then go into instant heavy drag mode. Matched with a stout two-handed rod, spinning has now proved itself up to the game of shiner fishing, even on the largest bass. Regardless of which outfit you use when casting shiner and bobber, the rhythm is necessarily slow, the cast a long, lobbing effort.

Perhaps toughest of all to learn in shiner fishing is when to hit a fish when you're using a float. Bass that hit a float-rigged golden shiner can do a number of things: swallow it immediately, grab it and run, crush it and blow it out several times, and a number of variations on these basic themes. The float reacts, naturally, and it will drive you crazy as it darts around when the shiner first realizes that a bass is in the neighborhood; or it will dance and kick, go under briefly, and then pop up again. Or maybe it will go under, move off a few feet, and then reappear. The rule of thumb is to wait it out. No matter how rattled you are, don't strike until you see that the float is under for good. The worst scenario of all is the float that disappears and doesn't resurface as a bass makes a long first run. The fish is beyond striking distance as it's marked on your line, and before you can close up, your float pops to the surface. Too many anglers assume that it's all over at this point. Not necessarily. Quickly move close enough for striking. Often, a bass has run with the bait to avoid one of his bigmouthed buddies trying to take away the meal. Once he feels safe, he'll often blow out the shiner once to position it for better swallowing. If you've done things correctly—you've not moved the bait and have closed within the magic 45-foot strike distance—and the float goes under one more time, sock him!

Once you've come through one of these little episodes, your itching trigger reflexes under control despite hands that are shaking like aspen leaves in the wind, you will have joined the ranks of a special group of bait anglers—the golden shiner fishermen.

Ultralight Largemouths

by Jim Dean

Who says that you're giving up chances at big bass by using light tackle? You could be handicapping yourself by not using it.

D ANGED IF IT WASN'T JUST LIKE one of those "good news, bad news" jokes. First, there was the good news. Jack Avent and I were sitting in the middle of the most incredible orgy of feeding largemouth bass that either of us had ever seen. The entire shallow cove at the head of the lake seemed to be awash with swirls, splashes and showers of escaping minnows.

We'd see an eruption along the edge of a large bed of lily pads, and suddenly, behind us, a dozen more largemouths would gang up for an assault in water barely 2 feet deep. It was wild and crazy, and we were casting like a couple of demons.

The bad news was that we couldn't get a strike on anything, and believe me, we were rooting through our tackle boxes like hogs digging sweet potatoes. We knew that the bass were feeding on schooling minnows. We'd even identified the minnows as golden shiners.

"The only way we're gonna get a bass to eat one of these plugs is if we personally stuff it in his mouth and rub his throat," complained Jack in utter frustration.

The problem was obvious. We had plenty of minnow imitations, but we were using heavy baitcasting outfits, and our lures were too big. Most of those shiners were small, and the bass were locked in on an abundance of 2-inch snacks. Anything larger looked unnatural and was ignored. When the nearly 3-hour feeding spree slacked off at dark, we wearily headed for home. Our total was three small bass, two of them foul-hooked.

The following day, we got a measure of revenge. When the first signs of feeding bass appeared, we were sitting in the middle of the cove armed with ultralight spinning rods and small floating/diving minnow imitations the same size as the shiners. I have never experienced faster fishing in my life. We later figured that we must have landed and released at least 20 bass apiece ranging from 1 to 4 pounds. At dusk, I lost a legitimate lunker that managed to pull free of the hooks in a mad dash.

That kind of fishing reveals the "good news, bad news" aspects of ultralight tackle. On the plus side, it demonstrates the value of ultralight spinning tackle as a legitimate and sometimes necessary angling tool for the serious angler. Nothing you can use, short of dynamite (or possibly live bait), will either outfish ultralight tackle for sheer numbers of bass, or eclipse the sheer joy of catching largemouths. Unfortunately, you also run a greater risk of losing a lunker, especially around cover. But you can also argue—and I will—that without ultralight tackle, you might not have hooked that whopper to begin with. Furthermore, your chances of landing a trophy on light line may be better than you think.

Of course, there's more to ultralight spinning for bass than just catching lots of bass, but let's not pass over that advantage too quickly. I don't know about you, but I occasionally need a payoff on my angling investment. How many days have you fished from dawn to dark and caught one or two bass? Or no bass? Doesn't it charge your battery once in a while to smoke 'em, even if most of the fish turn out to be less than 3 pounds?

Besides, who says that you're sacrificing a chance at a lunker largemouth just because you're using light tackle? More and more anglers are learning that there are times and conditions when an ultralight rod is far more than just a joystick for small fish. It's also sometimes the best medicine for big, wary bass.

One afternoon last spring, I had finished work early on the farm that I manage in my spare time and had about an hour of daylight left. A stock pond in a nearby pasture looked inviting, but I had only my ultralight spinning outfit with me. Because I didn't have a boat, I decided to simply walk around the shoreline and make a few casts before heading home.

Bass were on the move, and I caught several up to about 2 pounds using a Tiny Torpedo—a small surface lure with a rear prop. A large swirl near the bank ahead of me caught my eye, and I fired a cast in that direction. The lure was nearly at my feet when there came a savage strike. Because the bass was obviously strong enough to break the 4-pound mono I was using, I played it on a light drag. Several times, the fish made exciting runs, but I finally slid its head up the bank and lipped the 5-pound 13-ounce largemouth. Not a bad fish any day, and especially on such light tackle.

Ultralight spinning tackle is hardly new, but few serious bass fishermen have used it regularly until fairly recently. Back in the 1950s and early '60s, ultralight was all the rage among trout and panfish anglers, who snapped up the tiny imported spinning reels. Soon, domestic manufacturers were producing superb reels of their own. These little jewels were spooled with monofilament lines testing 1 to 4 pounds, and they were mounted on short, whippy glass or bamboo rods that were thought to be the best design for casting tiny spinners, jigs and plugs.

Such outfits had drawbacks, however, particularly for bass fishing. Anglers found it difficult to set the hooks with those short, soft rods. Even when they managed to set the hooks, the line was simply too light to stop any sizable bass from bulling its way into cover. Those noodly rods also tended to flex sideways when the angler cast, making it difficult to obtain the kind of accuracy necessary in most bass fishing.

Ultralight spinning tackle has undergone many improvements over the past few decades. Soft-action rods are still preferred by some fishermen who fish the tiniest lures weighing less than ⅛ ounce, but the newer graphite rods are far more versatile, and they handle a wider range of lure weights. Stiffer, longer and virtually weightless, these new rods cast farther and more accurately, and they set hooks better. And unless you're using a cobweb for line, you won't necessarily break off more fish with the stiffer rods.

Monofilament line for ultralight spinning has also improved—it's thinner, stronger and more limp. Indeed, 2-pound test is the lightest line now commonly available, and 4-pound mono has become the standard. With modern lines and graphite rods, anglers have a more versatile outfit that can be used for more species and under more conditions.

Equally important for bass fishermen are the developments that have been made in what I simply call light tackle. In recent years, manufacturers have introduced a superb array of rods and reels—both spinning and casting—designed to handle monofilament in the 6- to 8-pound range, and more and more bass fishermen are discovering that this gear fills a real gap between ultralight and heavy tackle.

I'll never forget my grandfather's reaction the first time he hooked a big bass on 6-pound-test spinning tackle. He'd been using heavy casting tackle for at least 40 years, but had begun using the spinning rod occasionally because I had given it to him, and also because the smaller lures caught more bass. He was a changed man after that big bass grabbed his diving minnow.

"I can't stop him," Grandpa wailed as the fish stripped off yards of line. Then, after the bass had made two spectacular jumps and another long run, my grandfather was able to land the 7-pounder.

"I've caught bigger bass, but that's the most fun I've ever had," he said as he admired his catch. Over the remaining years of his life, his old faithful casting outfit got less and less use, and light tackle had another convert.

This trend toward lighter tackle is little more than phenomenal when you consider that the line still preferred today on standard baitcasting and spinning rods tests anywhere from 10 to 30 pounds, with 20-pound test being the most popular choice for weighted plastic worms.

As you might expect, professional bass fishermen have led this charge toward lighter tackle and lines because they've learned that smaller lures are often far more effective than the big 3/8- and 5/8-ounce lures that have been the standard since the turn of the century. These smaller lures hit the water with less splash, and they spook fewer fish. Lures from 1/8 to 1/4 ounce also more closely approximate the size of many natural foods, and some—not all—have tighter, more enticing actions.

Even many standard-size lures—crankbaits, for example—dig deeper and have far better action on 8-pound test than they do on 20-pound mono. Spoons jigged in deep water also sink quicker and have better action on lighter lines, and switching to lighter line is a trick that many tournament fishermen use when threatening cover isn't a big problem.

Sure, you still need heavy tackle, stout lines and big lures, especially if you're fishing around stumps, snags, grass beds or other cover, but when heavy tackle is obviously not the best choice, somebody with lighter tackle is catching your fish.

When should you use ultralight or light tackle? And how? The bass will tell you, if you pay attention. There are, for example, predictable situations similar to the one Jack and I faced at the beginning of this story, and it's a pattern you can look for not only in the fall, but also each spring. In many lakes early in the spring, bass, before they begin spawning, often gather to feed on shiners or other baitfish over shallow flats. They return to the same pattern again in the late summer, and the action frequently lasts well into early winter. When those shallow, open-water patterns exist, light tackle is the ticket.

Schools of threadfin shad afford similar opportunities in big impoundments, not only in early spring when they gather along shorelines to spawn, but also throughout the summer and fall when they suspend in large concentrations over points or other structure. Bass that gather to chase threadfins or shiners are prime targets for small crankbaits or jigged spoons because the baitfish are usually fairly small, and hooked bass can be played safely on lighter lines.

Early last fall, Jack and I were having a mediocre day, and we couldn't seem to find any pattern to concentrate on. As we crossed the lake, my depth finder suddenly lit up, showing schools of bait and larger fish suspended over open water.

Perhaps because the water was only about 10 feet deep, the fish were spooky, and we were having trouble getting close enough to the schools without spooking them. But that wasn't the only problem.

"I think that our lures are bigger than the bait these bass are feeding on," said Jack. "Let's try smaller lures on ultralight. We'll also be able to cast farther, perhaps far enough to reach the fish without frightening them."

We tied on small sonic-type rattle plugs, and the rest—as they say—is history. Moving quietly and making long casts, we caught perhaps a dozen schoolies in the 2-pound class. Such conditions are by no means uncommon, and light tackle is often the solution.

There's another common situation that calls for lighter tackle and lines. Lots of times, if you're tossing big lures into gin-clear or slick, calm water, you might as well be tossing bricks. You're scaring fish, and if you don't believe it, try an experiment. Fish a stretch of shoreline with a big lure, then fish a similar stretch—or even the same one—with smaller lures that barely slap the water when they land. Guess which tactic catches the most bass?

These days, when I fish large impoundments, I carry not only a medium-weight spin or baitcasting rod for plugging and a heavier outfit for plastic worms, but I also carry an ultralight rig with 4-pound line or a light spinning outfit with 6-pound line. When I think that I may need it, I also carry a light casting or spinning rod with 8-pound line. One trip to a large lake late last spring proved the value of such diversity.

I began—as I often do—at daylight, fishing standard-size topwater lures along the shorelines with a medium-weight baitcasting rod; and I caught a couple of bass. As the sun burned off the morning fog, I moved to shallow flats in mouths of coves and switched to ultralight spinning tackle with 4-pound-test line and small crankbaits and spinnerbaits with soft-plastic bodies. I caught perhaps a half-dozen bass from 1 to 2 pounds before the action slowed around mid-morning.

My next stop was a deep bank, where I fished large, weighted plastic worms on my heavy baitcasting outfit. It was the best choice for that spot because I was probing the submerged tops of fallen trees, and I landed a 3-pound largemouth.

By mid-afternoon, I was working crankbaits over deep points and along a rocky riprap bank around a bridge. I used both a medium-weight casting outfit and a much lighter casting outfit with 8-pound test. I caught four bass, three of them on the light rig with small diving plugs. By late afternoon, I'd hit pay dirt again, this time in calm, clear water in the backs of several coves using a light spinning outfit with 6-pound test and small, shallow-diving plugs. I bagged a half-dozen decent bass, including one that went nearly 5 pounds—my best fish of the day.

In each case, I selected the tackle that was best suited to the situation,

ULTRALIGHT RODS AND REELS allow you to present tiny lures to finicky clear-water bass.

and it paid off in more bass of all sizes. Sure, I was carrying more gear, but it was a fair swap for versatility.

You are likely to encounter one minor problem when selecting lures for ultralight or light outfits. Some of these little lures have good action, but many do not, and some perform so poorly that it will make you wonder if the manufacturer ever tested them. Problems are more likely with lures weighing ⅛ ounce or less, but they are less evident in lures weighing 3/16 to 1/4 ounce. To some extent, you'll have to learn this by trial and error, but I may be able to help by listing types that work well for me.

Fortunately, you'll find that you need fewer different types of lures to cover most light tackle situations. One of the most versatile and reliable types is a 1/8- to 1/4-ounce safety-pin-style spinnerbait with a soft-plastic body. Few bass—or any other gamefish, for that matter—can resist these lures, and they can be fished at virtually any depth without hanging up. Small jigs, spoons and straight-shanked spinners also perform well and are effective.

Small crankbaits are among the most effective ultralight and light lures, but you'll encounter a wide variance in action—even among very similar models—and some simply don't work well. You're looking for lures that have a tight, quivering action and that run true without twirling and twisting your line. You'll notice that many small lures often require a much slower retrieve—some too slow to be truly effective. Even the best small lures tend to spin if you crank them too rapidly. Still, some of these small floating/diving minnow imitations are very effective.

Over the past 2 years, I've caught more bass in the 3- to 5-pound range on small crankbaits than on any other lure except plastic worms. During one brief period last year, I could have sold Jack a small chartreuse-and-blue crankbait for big bucks because it outfished everything else we had. After I caught a half-dozen bass—including one 4-pounder—on that crankbait one afternoon, Jack had had enough.

"Look, you've got two of those, haven't you?" he asked. "How about letting me borrow one of them?"

"Sure thing," I answered. I failed to mention, however, that although both lures appeared to be identical, one of them had poor action for some reason and tended to spin when retrieved. Of course, that's the one I loaned him, and after fishing it awhile, he seemed puzzled.

"I can't get it to work like yours," he complained.

"Here, try this one," I said, laughing. "That one's got a hex on it." We swapped lures, and after he landed a couple of nice bass while I was going fishless, it was clear that we had swapped luck.

Because I often work shallow-running crankbaits on the surface, I don't carry many purely ultralight or light topwater lures, although

I'll admit that a noisy little topwater lure with one or two propellers can be a killer.

I don't recommend that you try to fish plastic worms on 4- to 6-pound-test line. With so much line stretch, it's tough to set hooks even with stiffer graphite rods; however, you can effectively fish small worms on 8-pound test if you leave the hook point exposed and stay clear of heavy cover.

Sooner or later, you're almost certain to hook a big bass on light line, but you don't necessarily have to blow the lunker a goodbye kiss. Light line can be surprisingly tough because it stretches. Try to break it sometime when you get hung up. Still, it pays to take extra care when tying knots, and you should use a knot that retains close to 100 percent of the line test when properly tied. My favorite is the uni-knot.

Also, I frequently check the last few feet of line for nicks or abrasions, and I always do so after catching a fish. If there's any doubt, I cut off a few feet and retie the lure. It also pays to check your drag more frequently to make sure that it isn't too tight.

Even after you hook a big bass, there's a trick that may help you land it. If your fish burrows into a grass bed or ducks around a limb or stump, give it slack line. Often the fish will free itself, but if not, you can move the boat close enough to try to work the line off the obstruction. Even on slack line, bass have more trouble getting the leverage to free themselves from light lures; and those tiny, sharp hooks usually hold.

There's little advantage to owning one of the short rods most often associated with ultralight angling, unless you fish small, thickly canopied streams. For bass in lakes and ponds, longer casts are a real advantage, and longer rods will give you that distance. My favorite ultralight and light spinning sticks measure 6½ feet.

In these days of heavy fishing pressure and super-wary bass, you need all of the advantages you can get; and showing those bass a dainty little morsel often seems to whet their appetites when nothing else will.

Yep, it means carrying more gear, and heaven knows that most of us already carry plenty. But tell me, honestly, wouldn't you really like to "smoke'em" just once in a while? Thought so.

Summer Smallmouth Secrets

by Will Ryan

Smallmouths are a different kettle of fish after the spawn—so you need to fish differently to catch them.

WITH MULTI-COLORED PLASTIC worms, inch-thick fishing catalogs, and lure compendiums that pass as tackle boxes, largemouth anglers have the reputation as the compulsive shoppers of the bass fishing world. If the truth were known, however, it's smallmouth fishermen who are the real lure hounds. They just keep it in the closet— so to speak.

I know, because I always spend my winter searching for the perfect smallmouth lure. I did come close to finding it once, back during the 1950s. I was 8 years old, and the object of my affection was a French lure that was touted as the neatest thing since split-shot sinkers. It was called a Vivif, and it had a motorized tail. My friends and I never could figure out if you cast it or just let it free-spool.

That summer I met my first larger-than-life outdoorsman. His name was Don Wolfe, and he worked at a state park on the nearby St. Lawrence River. Don was a river man, tough as shoreline cedar, and he fished for bass every evening after work. Anglers would follow him, hoping to see how he did it, or at least where. Don never encouraged their company, of course. He cussed at them in fact, calling them tourists and even worse names than that in private. For some reason, he took pity on me.

"Never mind those damn motored lures," he growled at me on the docks one day when I asked him about the Vivif. "Come here, I'll show you what you need to catch those bass."

He reached into his bait bucket, pulled out a handful of crayfish and dumped them into an empty can. Then he handed it to me. He squinted at me and lowered his voice: "This is between you and me, now. Don't go telling everybody who fishes, especially those guys over in the next boat. I've got a bet with 'em on who catches the most bass. They think I'm catching 'em on a secret lure, which I am—sort of."

Then, as now, springtime bass took nearly any spinner, plug or spoon you threw at them, so it's easy to see how Don had everybody fooled. When the surface temperatures climb above 70°F, however, the smallmouths drift back to deeper water. They are a different fish with spawning season behind them. They spend much of their time in the 20- to 40-foot depths, and when they return to shallows to feed they want the real thing, not some facsimile.

Don Wolfe was right. When all of the new lures have been tried and discarded, when the corn stands tall and the summer sun blazes away in a cloudless sky, nothing catches smallmouth bass like live bait. And the best summer bait, for the most part, is a live crayfish. Studies show it to be far and away the preferred food of adult bass in the lakes, ponds and rivers in which it naturally occurs. Moreover, crayfish work in waters where they are not found naturally. I've yet to fish a smallmouth water that proved an exception.

Aquatic biologists will tell you that crayfish grow by molting, or shedding their shells. Molting occurs most frequently during their first year when their rate of growth is the fastest. Thus, young crayfish are most likely to be "soft-shelled." Biologists will also tell you that during molting, crayfish become particularly vulnerable to predators. Read: smallmouth bass.

You can gather crayfish with a minnow seine. You can collect lots of soft-shells because an age-class sometimes molts around the same time. (You can delay the hardening process by keeping them cool and out of water.) If you are like most of us in this day and age, though, you fish with what the guy at the bait shop has to sell. If you can't get soft-shells, go with the smaller hard-shells. If you have to travel any distance, don't keep them in water because they will deplete the oxygen and suffocate. Rather, just keep them in damp moss.

The bigger hard-shells become more appealing if you break off the front claws; if nothing else, it prevents them from grabbing the bottom. Hook the crayfish through the tail, and use as little weight as necessary to keep the bait near the bottom. Bass will pick up the crayfish as they would any other bait, move off a ways, then swal-

FISHING WITH LIVE CRAYFISH is a great way to catch big smallies consistently.

low it. The bigger the bait, the longer, in general, that the fish will run with it.

Crayfish seldom play second fiddle as a smallmouth bait during the summer months. The exception is in rivers and streams, where hellgrammites, the ugly looking larva of the dobsonfly, become king of the bass baits. Few stores carry them, and you may have better luck catching them yourself in fast stretches of streams. Have a friend hold a seine in the current and then turn over flat rocks a foot or so upstream, and hellgrammites (along with any crayfish or bottom-dwelling sculpin or madtoms) will wash into the waiting net. Hook the hellgrammite beneath its tough collar just behind its head, and drift it as if it was a night crawler.

The ubiquitous shiner, sold at bait stores throughout the country, probably catches as many bass as any other bait during the summer.

Night crawlers, crickets and small frogs will all provide fish at one time or another, as well. Indigenous baitfish—sculpin and madtoms come quickly to mind—can sometimes turn the trick when everything else fails.

The biggest smallmouth bass I ever hooked took an indigenous bait, though the whole encounter was as fluky as a summer breeze. I was fishing on tiny South Pond in northern Vermont and I'd casted, trolled and drifted for much of the morning with little success. Finally, I caught a small perch and, for lack of a better idea, rigged it beneath a bobber and lobbed the whole mess over by a brush pile. Instantly, the bobber plunged beneath the surface. I gave the fish—a pickerel, I presumed—a few minutes to chomp on the bait.

Five minutes was long enough for a pickerel, I figured, and I set the hook sharply. The line rose rapidly through the water and then, for a brief moment, I was eyeball to eyeball with what was (and still is) the largest smallmouth I've ever had on a line. The bass opened its mouth, though, and the hapless perch came sailing back over my shoulder. Five minutes may have been long enough for a pickerel, but not for this bass.

What tempted this fish? Indigenous bait? Presentation next to the brush pile? I honestly don't know, although it's not for lack of trying. Let me put it this way. I spent more than one summer evening over the years fishing 6-inch perch next to brush piles at South Pond. Never caught another bass (caught some nice pickerel, though) and learned in the process that catching summer smallmouths only begins with having the right bait.

Finding the bass is the important next step. Listen to old-time smallmouth anglers talk sometime. They revere their shoals; they sound like bird hunters talking about secret coverts. They know that summer smallmouths seldom stray from clear structure, a midwater shoal, for instance, that has baitfish hovering over the gravel or crayfish scuttling beneath the boulders. In smaller lakes and ponds, a deep shoreline or, in the case of South Pond, a brush pile or a blowdown comprises the prime spot.

Contrary to myth, smallmouths find themselves right at home in weed beds. During the summer months, they often seek out gravel patches bordered by weeds, even though the depths of such spots seldom reach 15 feet. Minnows and baitfish dart about in the grass, so the smallmouths move right in.

The offshore gravel and rock reef remains the traditional smallmouth fishing hole, however. My favorite smallmouth spot on New York's St. Lawrence River exemplifies such a shoal: A gravel and boulder shelf extends from an island and varies in depth from 18 to 25 feet, falling eventually to 50 feet and more of river channel. In essence, there are two islands, each the size of a football field. One reaches above the surface of the water, the other—the shoal—lays below. For centuries, the strong river currents and southwesterly winds have pounded against the head of the island and the front of the shoal, and for years the smallmouths have moved in there during the summer to gorge on crayfish and shiners.

This is also, I should point out, the spot where St. Lawrence bass wizard Don Wolfe mystified vacationers for so many summers. He caught smallmouths under any conditions, even as a high pressure system poised above the Canadian shore and a northwesterly wind threatened to dislodge your fillings. On those days, Don explained, the bait had to be drifted with light lines and small split shot. You had to throw it upriver so that it would "tick" back to you along the bottom. "Just like trout fishing," he'd say.

He was right, of course, and what he said holds true today. Many anglers tend to think of bait a little too literally—that it will actually draw bass as if they were so many catfish converging on a stinkbait. Smallmouths will sometimes take a bait anchored down by a heavy sinker, but they will nearly always take one drifting with current.

To do this, you need a fairly light line. Four-pound test is about right; six-pound makes sense if the water is weedy or holds pike. Use as little weight as possible and a No. 4 hook. In recent years, I've started using a 7-foot-long fly rod and taping a spinning reel to the handle. The sensitivity of this rig comes in handy on those sharp clear days when you need to fish your baits "trout-style." Try the smallest, softest crayfish in your bucket (or smallest shiner, or garden worm rather than crawler) and be prepared for light hits, perhaps even dropping down in hook size to a No. 6. If that doesn't work, try just the crayfish tail, peeling off part of the shell. Twitch it along the bottom. If this doesn't get a hit, nothing will.

And sometimes it won't because weather can really put the clamp on smallmouth fishing. A cold rain, for instance, can send the bass diving for the weeds.

A cold front is only one example of how weather can shut down bass fishing. Many years ago, while spending the summer on Lake Champlain in Vermont, I faced the opposite situation: sweltering heat. Gorgeous gravel shoals and points and islands provided nothing but bug-eyed rock bass; you know, the 5-inch kind that are three-quarters mouth and one-quarter tail. It had been blistering hot, and early morning, I realized with some reluctance, presented the only opportunity to catch a bass.

The next morning I was up before 5 a.m. and motored out to a gravel shoal. I cast out a live crayfish, left the bail of my spinning reel open, and turned to pour a cup of coffee from the thermos. I turned back around to the most pleasant sound a livebait angler hears: slack line whispering through the guides.

It was a good bass, as it turned out, and I caught a number of them before the sun hit the water. In mornings to come, I would catch fish farther back in the bay; one of my favorite spots was between the moorings of two big sailboats in less than 10 feet of water. Another great spot was a nearby pine-covered bluff, where the bottom fell to 30 feet or more.

That month on Champlain certainly convinced me of the power of first light during hot weather, but it also made me rethink one of the cannons of smallmouth lore: That during midsummer, the fish of any given body of water hold at one depth, and to catch them you must fish at *that* depth only. Those Lake Champlain bass held at various depths between 5 and 35 feet depending on the spot. That is, the depth of sailboat shoal, as I came to call it, was 8 feet, while the depth of pine tree point was 33. When they bit at one spot, they bit at the other. And when they stopped—which they did every day at 9 a.m. or so—they stopped biting everywhere, depth or no depth, crayfish or no crayfish.

Last year on Lake Ontario, the same thing happened. A friend and I did very well at first light off a deep-water spot where the water is 40 feet deep. Later that afternoon, with temperatures edging toward 90°, we caught fish over a gravel shoal in no more than 10 feet of water. On the way home, we stopped to get a soda at a bait store. The owner, when he learned of our good luck, said, "Yeah, a couple of other guys were in here just before you. They did real well, too, drifting in 25 feet, they said."

Now the point here is not that anglers should ignore the advice of bait-store owners. Nor is it that warm water drives bass into the shallows; generally, of course, it has the opposite effect. Rather, my point is that bass follow food, and my guess is that both Champlain and Ontario smallmouths found comfort and some food in the deep water, and discomfort but more food in the shallow gravel patches surrounded by weeds. Perhaps the bass moved on to these shallow spots, tolerated the 75° temperature briefly in return for easier pickings, and then moved off again.

No one knows for sure, of course, but one thing is clear: Finding smallmouths is more than fishing at the right depth. Drift fishing with live bait can really help in this regard, as you can cover an area more efficiently. The trick is to keep the bait within several feet of the bottom, and this means matching sinker weight to drift speed.

Drifting is more than just a way to find fish. Where the bottom slopes gently, drifting becomes a method in itself. Some anglers use it to enhance their presentation and simply drift repeatedly by an anchored buoy that marks the school. Al Benas, a well-known guide in the Thousand Islands, successfully drift-fishes with shiners in all kinds of situations. Lake Ontario guides often drift crayfish behind a sea anchor. The bouncing anchor stirs up cobblestones, dislodging crayfish, and you can guess what they attract.

Finally, smallmouths swim with schools of baitfish, and a drifted bait appears like a minnow trailing the school. Try removing the weight from your line, your anchor from the bottom, and drifting a live shiner just beneath the surface. The biggest smallmouth I've ever seen, in fact, was one my friend Pete Bellinger hooked just that way one hot July night many years ago. A silver chop broke the surface, but the moon was bright and you could see the great fish as it cleared the waves and spit the hook. It remains an indelible memory—and I was just watching.

Even today 20 years later, Pete will turn to a weightless shiner right about dusk and cast and retrieve it, or if we're drifting, toss it out and let it ride the waves. Hoping, waiting. . . .

He's yet to drive the hook into a bass of that size. But if you ask me, he's going about it in the right way because live bait will nearly always put some bass on the stringer, and often when nothing else will. Don Wolfe was right; live bait is the secret to summer smallmouths.

But whatever you do, don't tell those guys in the next boat.

Clickin' Brass for Bass

by Bob McNally

A simple refinement in the rigging of soft plastic lures is raising a clamor among fishermen nationwide.

IT WAS THE KIND OF spring morning that makes a bass fisherman sing. The sun was just tipping over the eastern horizon, its light filtering through tall, dew-glistening cypress trees heavy with Spanish moss. The flat surface of the St. Johns River near where I live in northeastern Florida reflected the sun's brilliant orange and red colors. It was a spectacular dawn fishing scene I'd witnessed hundreds of times before on my home water, but on this particular morning it had never looked better.

That's because my two sons, 10-year-old Eric and 7-year-old Matt, were "guiding" me for bass in their new 14-foot boat. We'd fished that part of the St. Johns together for bass often, but this was the first outing for the boys in their new johnboat. They were anxious to show Dad they were adept at finding and catching largemouth bass around the hundreds of docks, piers and pilings that line the river's shores south of Jacksonville.

Our first fishing stop was the "church dock," a long, half-circle pier that had dozens of crossbeams and old pilings below it in water 8 feet deep. It had produced many largemouths for us over the years and was a top daybreak choice.

"What are you gonna use, Dad?" asked Matt.

"Brown tube lure with a brass slip weight and glass bead," I said, smiling.

"Okay, I'll fish a spinnerbait," Matt replied in a thoughtful tone.

"I'll try a topwater plug," Eric stated with conviction.

Eric eased the little boat along the outside edge of the church dock pilings, and I dropped my 3-inch-long tube lure beside a crossbeam support far back under the dock. My line went slack when the lure settled on sunken pilings. Then I gave a soft, subtle shake with the rod handle and felt the tube and brass slip weight tumble and fall through more cross beams. With my sensitive graphite rod I could feel the brass weight "clicking" and "clacking" against the glass bead ahead of the tube as the lure plummeted helter-skelter toward the bottom.

The line went slack again. I gave the rod another shake and felt a solid "thump" that only a taking bass can deliver.

"Got one," I told my guides as I took slack out of the line and set the hook hard and fast.

Water boiled and churned under the church dock from the battling bass as I leaned against the fish with my rod all I dared, horsing it to open water. A rod length away from the boat, eye level in front of Matt, the fish jumped.

"Wow!" he hollered. "Get the net, it's a monster!"

Eric already had the net in hand, and a few seconds later I eased the 7-pounder into the mesh and Eric quickly plucked it from the water. After a couple of photographs the bass was released unharmed.

Eric repositioned the boat near the dock, and we fired casts to pilings again with the kind of vigor only a hefty bass can instill in early morning anglers. A few casts later, following another shake of the rod, I hooked and landed a 3-pound bass. Then I caught a pair of smaller fish and a 4-pounder—all by shaking the glass-and-brass-fitted tube lure.

"I want a tube lure, Dad," declared Matt.

"Me, too," said Eric.

I quickly rigged the boys' rods with soft plastic tubes, brass slip weights and small glass beads. The bright, gold-colored, bullet-shaped brass slip weights slid onto the fishing lines like standard lead weights. Then salmon-egg-size red glass beads were positioned between the weights and hooks.

"The key to fishing a glass-and-brass lure, guys, is to shake or wiggle the rod after the lure hits bottom," I explained to my wide-eyed sons. "That makes the brass weight click loudly against the glass bead, which is a dinner bell sound to bass."

After a few minutes of cast-and-retrieve practice the boys had the technique down pat, and at the next dock we fished they each caught a bass with their tube lures. Through the morning we had good fishing with the tubes, and just to prove that glass and brass made a difference in the rig, I fished a tube lure for an hour using a standard lead slip sinker and no glass bead. I never caught a bass with it, though the boys boated five largemouths using the identical lure rigged with glass and brass.

That such a subtle difference in lure rigging and presentation can create a dramatic difference in bass catching success may seem like hyperbole in this era of overstated bass fishing techniques. But during the past year I've become convinced that most soft plastic lures—worms, tubes, grubs, crayfish, eels and lizards—can be made much more effective for bass when they're used with brass slip weights and glass beads. This holds especially true in difficult bass fishing situations.

When bass are aggressive and actively feeding, anglers can get away with sloppy presentations and unrefined lure techniques. But when bass are deep, spooky, lethargic or heavily pressured, sophisticated tactics are needed for consistent success.

Rattling, sound-producing lures are old hat in the tackle industry. In fact, rattling has become almost a standard component for many plug designs, especially subsurface lures like crankbaits. Most of today's hollow plastic plugs make noise because they have lead shot sealed inside that rattles when the lures are retrieved. But making a solid, soft plastic lure rattle is much more difficult than getting a hard, hollow plug to emit sound.

Some companies manufacture hard plastic or metal capsulelike sound chambers. Lead shot is sealed inside the chamber, which can be inserted into soft plastic lures. Such rattling capsules do emit sound, but they are not as loud, nor as sharp sounding, as the clearly audible clicking a large brass slip weight makes when it strikes a glass bead.

Over the years, some tackle companies have produced hollow plastic cones that have lead slip weights inside. These, too, produce sound when used with soft plastic lures. But lead and plastic are very poor sound producers compared with glass and brass.

Glass-and-brass rigs are especially valuable when working dark, off-colored waters and when fishing at night. I'm convinced that bass most fully utilize their abilities to hear when they are less able to see their prey.

BRASS AND GLASS make a sound bass can't resist.

Tournament bass angler Rob Kilby of Hot Springs, Arkansas, agrees that sound is an important attraction for bass. That's why he's been a proponent of using glass and brass for several years.

"I learned about using glass and brass on big Western impoundments," says the six-time B.A.S.S. Masters Classic qualifier. "Guys out West were consistently catching suspended bass in 20 to 50 feet of water on 4- to 6-pound-test line. They used small 3/16-ounce brass slip weights, little glass beads and 5-inch plastic worms. Deep, suspended bass are some of the most difficult fish to catch, and they only could get 'em with plastic worms using glass-and-brass rigs.

"Those deep Western reservoir bass suspend off ledges. So you make a cast, let the glass-and-brass lures sink all the way to bottom, then with the boat's electric motor, pull the lure off the ledge without letting out any more line. This keeps the lure at the exact depth for fish suspended off structure. While you're moving the boat with the electric motor, you shake the rod tip, which causes the brass weight to 'pop' loudly against the glass bead ahead of the plastic worm. The clicking sound really draws bass. Some anglers say it's a perfect imitation of a crayfish snapping its pincers, or identically mimics the noise a crayfish makes as it swims while contracting its hard-shell tail. I don't know why the sound of glass and brass turns on bass, but it does."

After learning the Western glass-and-brass technique for deep suspended bass, Kilby applied it successfully to shallow brushtops and flooded timber. He uses larger soft plastic lures, heavier brass slip weights and bigger glass beads under these conditions.

"When you cast a plastic worm or lizard rigged with glass and brass into a treetop, and shake it so it pops and clicks, bass just annihilate it. They really zero in on that sound. The brass weight and glass bead create a sharp, distinct sound that's much more effective than any clicking sound chamber that can be added to a soft plastic lure. A lead sinker and a plastic bead don't have anywhere near the same resonance as glass and brass.

Glass-and-brass rigging can enhance the performance of practically any soft plastic bait, from tail worms and crayfish to grubs and tubes.

"There's no question that glass-and-brass rigging is the way to go with soft plastic lures. I've even fished behind other top tournament anglers and caught bass with a glass-and-brass rig where they had no success using standard lead slip sinkers. And I've had it work well for largemouths, smallmouths and spotted bass."

During a smallmouth bass trip last summer on Lake Erie, out of Strongsville, Ohio, I had exceptional smallmouth bass fishing with guide Bob Collins of Omni Charters. We fished deep rock piles and humps near Pelee Island, located just over the Canadian border. Deep, slow fishing with small Lindy Fuzz-E-Grub bodies rigged onto small exposed hooks, and fished with a glass-and-brass setup, proved most effective.

In 2 days of fishing we caught dozens of smallmouths this way, and we boated plenty of bass in the 3- to 4-pound class. We also caught several large walleyes using the same glass-and-brass rig, including a chunky 6-pounder by Collins. I'm convinced that the clicking sounds of glass and brass, used with the Lindy grubs, made our lures perfect crayfish imitations.

Glass and brass can be rigged effectively in many ways with soft plastic lures. For example, some anglers improve on the standard

Texas worm rig by using two or three glass beads with alternating brass weights. They reason that if one brass weight and glass bead are good for producing bass attracting sounds, several beads and weights are better. The Top Brass Tackle company manufactures small brass disks called Carolina Tickers that are ideal for such multi-weight rigging.

Top Brass also makes a wide array of colored brass slip weights and glass beads. Some anglers prefer sinker and bead colors identical to the hue of their plastic lure.

I like gaudy, shiny brass weights, however, because I believe their reflection helps attract bass, especially in clear or shallow water. A standard dull lead slip sinker is clearly outclassed by a brass weight in this regard.

Another plus for brass is its relative hardness. Fishing line holes drilled through brass weights are very precise and maintain their shape. Unlike a lead weight's hole, a brass hole will not pinch closed during normal fishing. An out-of-round hole in a lead slip sinker can cut, fray and damage fishing line. And lost lead weights are an environmental concern for some anglers, who for this reason opt for brass weights.

The Carolina rig is one of the best methods for using soft plastic lures, and glass-and-brass Carolina rigging components are becoming very popular. Jawtec Worms Inc. manufactures a special line of Carolina rigging kits, all of which are made with glass-and-brass parts.

With a Jawtec glass-and-brass Carolina kit, an angler first threads his fishing line through a large, cone-shaped, heavy brass slip sinker (1/2 or 3/4 ounce). Next, a glass bead or two is threaded onto the fishing fine, then the line is tied to one ring of a brass barrel swivel. A 2- to 6-foot leader is then tied to the opposite end of the swivel, and the plastic lure and hook are attached to the leader end.

The beauty of a Carolina rig is that its heavy weight kicks up a ruckus along the bottom, while a floating plastic lure on the leader hovers above weeds, rocks and muck to catch bass attracted to the bottom disturbances.

Bruce Benedict, owner of Jawtec, is an expert at Carolina rig-fishing. He always uses at least two glass beads with his brass rig sinker for added sound. He also says that when fishing hard, flat bottoms for bass, such as reservoir roadbeds, sandbars and clay banks, it's best to use a brass Carolina rig weight that has a large, blunt nose. Its shape bumps along the lake or river floor, creating bass attracting noise as it strikes against the glass beads. When fishing thick weeds, stump flats and flooded timber, Benedict uses a cone-shaped brass weight because it resists fouling.

A glass-and-brass rig also works well in current. In fact, the rig may be even more lethal for bass in rivers than in lakes and ponds. In moving water, a soft plastic lure fitted with glass and brass tumbles and rolls along the bottom, and the lure's clicking and clacking sound intensifies.

Finally, maybe the best reason of all to use glass and brass with soft plastic lures was made by a guy I met in a South Carolina tackle shop.

"Heck, why not use 'em?" he said firmly. "Sure doesn't cost much more for a brass slip weight and a glass bead for worm fishin' compared to a plain ol' lead weight. And it's just as easy to rig. When I figure what it costs to go bass fishing in time, gas, boat expense, rod and reel prices and other things, paying a few extra pennies to use brass slip weights and glass beads means nothin'.

"I have so much already tied up in bass fishing, I can't afford *not* to use glass and brass."

Trolling: Banned for Bass

by John E. Phillips

If you happen to be a professional bass tournament angler, stop reading. The following killer bass fishing method is not for you!

F ORGET FOR A FEW MOMENTS THE tactics that professional bass anglers tout for catching prized largemouths and smallmouths. There is one method they can't endorse, mainly because it's off-limits to the pros. And it very well could be the most effective way to take bass—period.

It's trolling, a method so good that it's been banned by most professional bass tournament organizations. In fact, in the Bass Anglers Sportsman Society (B.A.S.S.) tournament regulations, rule No. 9 clearly states: "Trolling as a method of fishing is prohibited." So that leaves it to us amateurs to capitalize on this simple, yet sure-fire method of hooking lunkers nearly every time out.

"I encourage all my clients to troll because trolling consistently produces more bass than casting and retrieving does," said Jack Wingate, nationally known bass fishing guide on Lake Seminole near Bainbridge, Georgia. "Regardless of age or skill level, fishermen can catch bass on most days they troll."

Wingate trolls artificial lures for bass. However, trolling is just as effective for live-bait fishermen.

"I troll live shiners during the winter months to cover more water and catch bigger bass," explained Buck Bray, a professional bass fishing guide on the Withlacoochee River near Dunnellon, Florida.

I discovered this bassing technique as a 5-year-old, fishing with my Dad in a boat made of cypress that we rented for 50¢ a day. The boat was powered by the fastest motor on the river at that time—a Wizard 3½ hp. Using an iron rod and braided nylon line, we trolled Bomber Mud Bugs with 18 inches of 12-pound-test leader tied to the last hook and a silver spoon attached on the end of the leader. All day long we trolled the banks of the Warrior River, close to my home in central Alabama, and caught numbers of bass, a few crappies and an occasional catfish. The same strategy would undoubtedly work today.

Bottom Walking

A highly productive tactic involves a trolling rig such as the Gapen Bait-Walker, which is simply a piece of lead attached to two spinnerbait-like wires. The bottom wire holds the lead. On the top wire, a piece of leader about 2 feet in length is attached and a variety of lures can be used: a crankbait, live bait, an in-line spinner or a jig. Slowly trolled, this rig keeps the bait near or on the bottom and in the bass' strike zone. To fish higher up off the bottom with the Bait-Walker rig, use a floater/diver type lure such as the Rebel Silver minnow, the Rapala minnow, the Wiggle Wart or any similar crankbait. Using this rig, anglers can troll a bait at almost any depth of water.

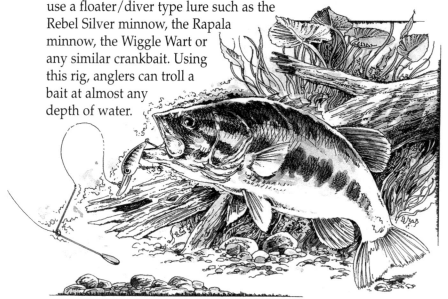

Trolling Points and Banks

Any expert will tell you that when starting out on a lake or river you've never fished before, the best spots to fish for bass are along points. Using trolling tactics, you can fish every segment of water on points and locate bass.

Begin trolling at the deepest end and the deepest sides of the underwater point using deep-diving crankbaits (A). Bagley's DB-3, Mann's 30+ and Double Deep Rebels are good choices. If the points are rocky, tie 18 to 20 inches of 8- to 12-pound-test line to the back hook of the crankbait. Attach a small, in-line spinner like the Mepps, Panther Martin or Rooster Tail to the other end of the line. Using this trailer rig, you double your odds of taking smallmouth, largemouth and/or spotted bass by presenting the fish with two different sizes and colors of lures.

Next move up to the middle of the point (B), and troll medium-depth crankbaits. Finally, go into the shallow water close to the bank (C), tie on your shallow-running crankbaits and troll. As you move into shallow water, you can eliminate the trailer lure.

Similarly, riverbank trolling (D) is one of the best ways to locate big bass that may be holding on structure so small a depth finder won't show it. But trolling banks is not only a tactic for taking bass in natural rivers; this technique also catches plenty of bass in large impoundments when you troll the edges of the underwater riverbanks as well as the shorelines.

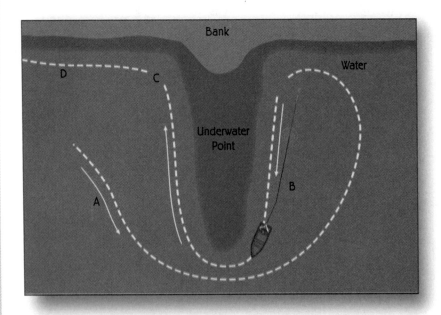

18-inch Leader

Deep-diving
Crankbait

Spoon

Bottom

Deep Trolling

Even in clear, highland reservoir lakes and the deep, clear lakes of the West, trolling a deep-diving crankbait with a trailer lure such as a silver spoon or any in-line spinner will produce largemouth, smallmouth and spotted bass.

One of the problems associated with catching bass in these deep, clear lakes is that bass often hold in the underwater caves and cracks in the sheer rock bluffs. If you cast to the bank, your bait falls away from the region where the bass are holding. However, when you troll in front of those bluffs, the bass in these underwater caves, cracks and caverns have time to see your bait, come away from their ambush points and attack the lure.

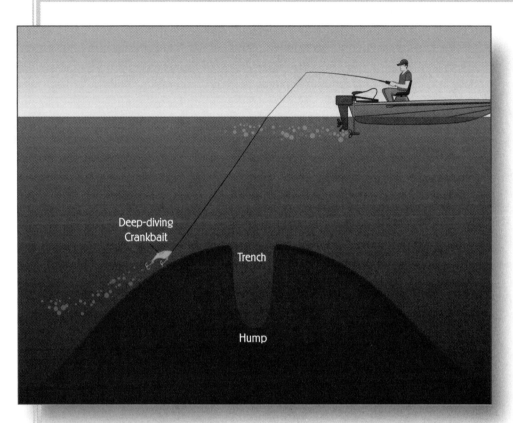

Deep-diving Crankbait

Trench

Hump

Trolling Humps

Other good trolling areas in any lake are humps. In many sections of the country, underwater humps in man-made reservoirs actually are Indian mounds left from the earliest days of our country. Before the reservoirs were inundated, archaeological teams often dug large trenches through the mounds to learn about the people who lived in these regions.

Today, bass concentrate in these underwater trenches through the mounds and wait to attack baitfish. Trolling deep-diving crankbaits puts a lure down on the mounds. When the bait passes over the trench, the bass will often come out and attack. Trolling the outside edges of these areas will also produce bass.

Vegetation Trolling

If you're on a lake or a river filled with aquatic vegetation, try trolling live bait. Large minnows, golden shiners and other big bait-fish trolled along the edges of the grass will pull big bass out of their hiding spots.

"I use a weedless hook and lip hook the shiners," Buck Bray advises. "Then I troll slowly along the edges of lily pads, peppergrass, hydrilla, milfoil and other kinds of water weeds to catch big bass."

When a bass hits the minnow, don't immediately set the hook. A large, live bait often will be taken sideways in the bass' mouth, so you must give the fish time to fully take the bait. Instead, point the rod straight at the bass and when the line tightens, then set the hook.

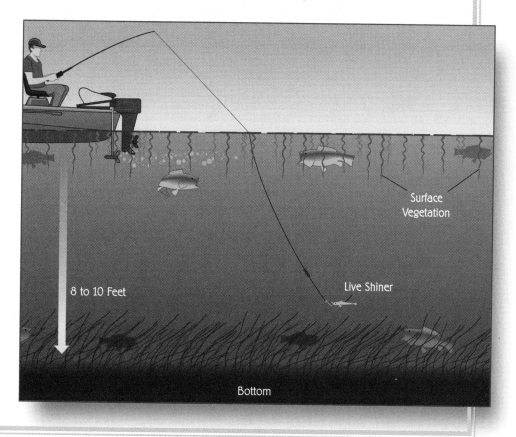

Surface Vegetation

8 to 10 Feet

Live Shiner

Bottom

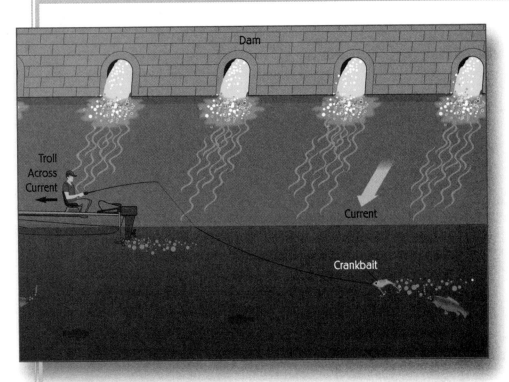

Trolling Tailrace

Tailrace areas below dams generally hold the largest concentrations of fish in any reservoir. In cool-water reservoirs, you'll frequently find big smallmouths as well as largemouths holding in the tailraces.

John Hill, a smallmouth specialist who fishes the tailrace at Wheeler Dam near Town Creek, Alabama, explains, "Smallmouth bass either will hold close to the dam or well away from the dam in a tailrace area. But locating smallmouths can be difficult, depending on how many turbines are running.

"I troll a Model A Bomber back and forth across the current from near the dam to a quarter mile below the dam. Using this tactic, I can pinpoint smallmouths and consistently catch them by trolling."

Selecting Speed

During the winter months the metabolism of bass slows down, so the fish will not chase baitfish as readily as in the spring and summer. For this reason, slow trolling either live baits or artificial lures often will produce more bass in the winter months than any other method.

In the spring and fall, when bass feed much more actively and are willing to chase baits, fast-trolled crankbaits such as Cotton Cordell's Spot lures or Bill Lewis' Rat-L-Traps often produce the most bass.

By changing the speed at which you troll, you also can vary the segment of water through which lures pass. Early in the morning when the bass are shallow, fast troll and use a long rod held straight up to keep lures such as a Rat-L-Trap in the shallow water where the bass are feeding. Later in the day slow troll. Not only reduce the speed of your trolling motor, but also lower the rod tip, keeping the rod parallel to the water.

So remember, trolling is a deadly tactic and can be employed at any time of the year on almost any body of water. It allows you to fish many segments of the water, while varying your strategies according to the wind, weather and water conditions. If you want to catch more bass, try trolling. The pros most certainly would—if they were allowed.

As the Worm Churns

by Bob McNally

They look wacky but don't be fooled: Swimming worms are deadly on bass, and they're easy to use.

KAREN DAVIS WAS ON A MISSION for her kids, and I was the target. "My son and daughter want to learn to fish, and you gotta teach me so I can teach them," she said. So one afternoon I took Karen and her kids out on our Florida boat dock for a quick, on-the-water lesson. I rigged a spinning outfit with a Little Mac swimming plastic worm, the easiest-to-use lure I could

think of, and gave her a few seconds of instruction. Her first cast sent the lure straight up 20 feet, and it landed in a coiled heap beside her on the pier. She laughed at her pratfall, and her daughter kicked the lure into the water.

Looking over the side, I watched it corkscrew into the clear river depths. As the worm churned toward the bottom, a huge bass darted out of the dock's shade and pounced on it. I told Karen to quickly wind the reel handle, and she promptly barbed the fish.

What followed is kind of a blur. There was lots of shouting, arm and hand waving, stomping of feet, and plenty of protest-splashing from the bass. But somehow Karen battled the largemouth to the surface, and I landed the 6-pounder for her.

As you might expect, Karen and her kids are now dedicated anglers, and they're devoted to fishing with swimming plastic worms.

Despite regular tales about the worm's effectiveness, most veteran bass fishermen are reluctant to use rigged swimming worms. What turns off most modern bass anglers to using swimming plastic worms is that the lures look much like the original rubber worms of 40 years ago. Further, contemporary bass fishermen have preconceived notions about what today's plastic worm should look like, and the bulk of sophisticated anglers don't want hooks, leaders and swivels rigged to their worms.

You can't really blame them. Shaped more like a road-kill snake than a modern plastic lure, a swimming worm doesn't garner much respect. With its goofy, curved body, rigged hooks, and outlandish colors, the swimming worm is more likely to be seen hanging from the end of a spincast rod owned by a 12-year-old kid than a Ricky Clunn wanna-be in a $30,000 bass boat. But the slow, tantalizing spin of a Z-shaped swimming worm is often more appealing to fish than traditional plastic worms. And because swimming worms have their own built-in action, they can't be fished incorrectly. Anyone who can cast and retrieve the rig will catch bass—as Karen Davis and her children will attest to.

And the worm's unpopularity actually works in its favor. You see, the swimming worm is so out of step with modern plastic worm designs that the majority of today's bass anglers have no idea what these remarkable bass-catching lures are all about. Because it's not used much, most fish have never seen the lure's remarkably different action. Bass that recognize standard plastic worms as phonies will be eager to strike the enticing newcomer.

The unique, purposefully molded C, S or Z-shape of a swimming plastic worm causes the lure to spin erratically as it is retrieved. Some worms spin in tight, fast circles; others spiral in wide, slow ovals. Their round-and-round action requires that they're fished with a quality ball-bearing swivel tied ahead of the lure. Without a swivel they'll tangle fishing line in just a few casts, and that makes for fouled lines on reels and rod guides.

Swimming or "spinning" soft-plastic worms are available in an array of colors, many in wild hues that are especially productive for clearwater bass. The worms vary from 3-inch models that tempt smallmouths and even chunky panfish, to giant 12-inchers that score on oversize Florida and California bass.

Most swimming worms are rigged with two or three hooks buried inside their soft-plastic bodies. The number and size of the hooks are determined by the length and thickness of the worm. Lures 6 inches or longer often have three single hooks that ensure barbing of even

SWIMMING WORMS can be fished in several basic ways. The worm is fished through weeds and stumps using a stop-and-go retreive. (It can be rigged with or without a small bullet-head sinker).

USING A SLIP SINKER, the worm can be fished deep and weedless over structure.

RIGGED CAROLINA-STYLE, the worm is fished with a vertical presentation over likely bass hangouts.

light-striking bass. Long worms are rigged with a hook at the head, one in its center and a third hook at the tail.

To facilitate good swimming action, often a smaller, lighter wire hook is used at the lure's tail. The little tail hook frequently is the one that barbs reluctant, hard-to-catch bass in clear water or hard-pressured lakes and rivers. These fish are well-known "nippers," the kind of shy bass that just nip the tails of standard-rig plastic worms without becoming hooked.

The swimming worm's rigged hooks are connected by 10- to 30-pound-test monofilament, with the line and hook shanks molded inside the plastic worm body. Most prerigged worms have monofilament extending from the forward hook, out the nose of the lure, forming a leader 1 to 3 feet long. Leader ends are tied in a loop for easy attachment to a ball-bearing snap swivel. Hook bends and points are exposed out the side of the worm body. Weedless and non-weedless hook models are available in different swimming worm styles.

No lure is better suited for bass in shallow, grassy water than a swimming worm rigged with weedless hooks. Even without weight added, a swimming worm can be cast a long way with spinning tackle. By using a stop-and-go retrieve through weeds, lily pads, stumps or brush tops, the spiraling worm unnerves bass.

A bullet-shaped slip weight also can be rigged onto a swimming worm's leader to get the lure deep, thereby burrowing weedlessly through grass, brush and other tangles.

A small swimming worm is one of my favorite soft-plastic baits for use in strong river currents. The lure is especially deadly for small-mouths. Most of the time I'll fish a 4-inch swimming worm and attach just enough split shot to the leader to get it down. An upstream cast is normally best, and the lure is fished slowly as it swings deep in the current—similar to how a flyfisherman works a nymph or streamer for trout. No action need be imparted to a swinging swimming worm because river current activates the lure in a swirling fashion most smallmouths go wild over.

Last summer on Idaho's Snake River I had great success on small-mouths tightlining 4-inch, all-brown swimming worms. Once, casting to a single large boulder, I landed 11 smallmouths weighing up to 3 pounds by swinging swimming worms around the rock. I'd cast 20 yards upstream of the boulder and allow the worm to sink, spiraling into the Snake's depths. By retrieving line a bit, or moving my rod tip left or right, I could direct the spinning worm right under the boulder's overhangs where smallmouths were stacked like a pack of wolves guarding their lair.

A Carolina-rigged swimming-worm—fished on a 4-foot leader ahead of a heavy slip sinker—is one of the greatest searching bass lures of all time. I fish it from a slow-moving boat, either pulled along by an electric motor, or when making a controlled wind drift over deep structure. The lure is cast out, allowed to sink to the bottom, and the boat is then moved along humps, channel edges, weed lines, drop-offs, rock piles and other structure. The lure is fished almost under the boat in a nearly vertical presentation. Worked this way I can keep a close watch on my depth finder to keep the lure in precise position on, say, a deep rocky "finger" or projection, or right on a weedy drop-off.

Sometimes when fish are spotted on my depth finder suspended off structure, I stop the boat and actively shake the Carolina rig. This causes the rig's heavy sinker to thump the bottom loudly and sends up bottom sediment that can draw bass. This also imparts up-and-down movement to the swimming worm, making it spin and wiggle. A remarkable number of big, deep-holding bass have fallen for that tactic, including an 8-pound largemouth I caught in South Carolina's Santee-Cooper Reservoir. Interestingly, fishing the same way with a black, 12-inch Little Mac swimming worm, I caught a 13-pound striped bass from the same reservoir structure the day after I caught the heavy black bass.

Two bass weighing a total of 21 pounds in two days is impressive for any lure fished by any technique. But I've learned not to be too surprised by the size, number and type of bass that swimming worms produce. It's simply a lure that rarely fails, in bass water coast to coast.

Bass: The Fly-Rod Advantage

by Jim Dean

Believe it: Flyfishing gear can be your best bass fishing weapon.

⌇

CHECK OUT THE ROD SELECTION on the boats around you next time you're waiting in line at a launching ramp. Clamped on the decks are so many casting, flipping, pitching, cranking, yanking and spinning, sticks that you'd swear someone had clear-cut a graphite forest. But is there ever a single fly rod to be seen? "I'm after bass, not a bunch of pint-size panfish," one fisherman told me. "I don't have room for toys." Probe a little deeper, and you'll get a raft of reasons, some that make

sense and some that are adrift in myth and misconception. Many dedicated flyfishermen even stumble when asked why they insist on using a fly rod for bass. "Well, it's just more fun," they're likely to say. But ask them to name one practical task a fly rod will perform better than casting or spinning tackle, and few can answer. Let's be honest. The purely pragmatic bass fisherman who wants the best tool for each task is better off using casting or spinning tackle most of the time. For example, a fly rod is a poor tool for probing deep summer structure even with the most modern, fast-sinking fly lines. Baitcasting and spinning tackle are almost invariably superior for bass any-time you're fishing more than a few feet deep, especially on big, open water. It's a chore to flycast into the wind all day, and there are limits to the maximum size and weight of fly or bug even the most powerful fatline sticks will handle.

But hold on a minute. If fly rods are so impractical, what explains the incredible boom in trout and saltwater flyfishing in recent years? And why are so many serious bass fishermen, the guys on the leading edge, also adding fly rods to their arsenal? The truth is, there are some tasks a fly rod can perform better than any other tackle. Let's take a closer look at ways a fly rod can give bass fishermen—perhaps even tournament pros—an edge.

Brute Force

A fly rod is the only tool that can deliver a small, fly-weight lure on really strong line. Ultralight spinning tackle can't even do that. Yet, the myth lingers that flyfishing demands light leaders. Who says? Sure, light leaders are sometimes necessary, but your leader and tippet can be as heavy as need be. If you're flyfishing around dense weeds, lily pads or tangled timber, there's no reason why you can't use a monofilament tippet that tests 20, 30 or even 40 pounds to haul those lunkers out of cover. Indeed, stronger, stiffer leaders will turn over big, heavy flies better than light leaders, and because bass are seldom leader-shy, why take chances? Even in open water, heavier tippets will let you land fish more quickly so that you can release them with a better chance of survival. For bass, I normally use a 10-foot leader tapered to 12- to 15-pound test, but I'll go to heavier tippets when I need them.

You might be surprised at how often the combination of a small bug or fly and a stout leader can work miracles on bass that might otherwise go uncaught. Last summer on Florida's vast Lake Okeechobee, following the 27th Annual Harold DeTar Flyfishing Tournament, guide Chris Rivers and I decided to do a little experimenting. The weather was so

PARTS OF A FLY ROD

Reel seat   Grip   Hookkeeper

Ferrule (female)

hot that bass fishing had been erratic, but I was curious to see if I could wake up the fish with bigger casting lures and plastic worms.

Late that afternoon, Rivers located bass chasing small minnows along the edge of one of Okeechobee's famed horizon-to-horizon beds of waterlilies. I had no luck at all with buzzbaits or other big lures, but Rivers borrowed one of my fly rods and caught nice bass on nearly every cast. It didn't take me long to grab another fly rod and join the fun.

The pads were far too thick and tough for ultralight spinning tackle, but with 20-pound-test tippets we could cast our minnowlike poppers fearlessly and drag fish into open water. It was particularly nice to have those heavier tippets because I knew that Rivers had caught a bass that weighed more than 8 pounds in the same spot a week earlier.

Splat, They're Outta Here

How do you handle clear, calm water and bass that spook like dirt-road lizards when your standard casting or spinning lure hits the water with the subtleness of a cinder block? If you've got a fly rod on board, it will delicately deliver small, nearly weightless enticements. By aiming your cast above the water's surface, your fly line will uncurl in midair and the bug or fly will drop to the surface like a feather (which, in many cases, it is).

Of course, you could use ultralight spinning tackle and small, light lures, and that's what many bass fishermen choose. And yet, a modern graphite fly rod in the hands of a skilled angler can actually cast farther and more accurately than most ultralight spinning outfits.

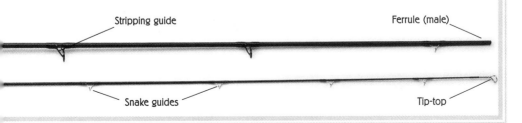

Stripping guide

Ferrule (male)

Snake guides

Tip-top

CHOOSE A GOOD-QUALITY weight-forward or bass-taper floating line that matches the weight of your rod. These lines are thicker on the fly end of the taper, providing the weight and power to cast heavy, wind-resistant bass flies. For backing, use 20- to 30-pound braided Dacron. You'll rarely get into it when bass fishing, but you should use it to fill your reel to keep your fly-line coils larger and limper. Literature included with your reel will tell you how much to use. For leaders, you'll find that stiff monofilament will turn over a fly better than the super-limp stuff. Your leader doesn't have to be overly long—7 to 10 feet is sufficient. Most of the knotless tapered leaders available are excellent and hassle-free. Tippets should test 10 to 15 pounds.

Pinpoint Accuracy

There are times when it's vital to deliver a lure to a small target cast after cast. Some highly skilled baitcasters can do it, but it's far easier with a fly rod. Even a flycaster with moderate skills can routinely cast a bug or fly 70 feet or more and place it within inches of a target. Such accuracy is essential when probing small pockets in emergent weed beds, lily pads or similar cover.

Two-Timing

With flyfishing gear, you can easily fish two flies at the same time— one on top and another running a couple of feet beneath the surface. It's not practical with casting or spinning tackle, but a fly rod can handle this chore easily. I frequently fish two flies for bass—panfish and trout, too—and usually choose a floating bug trailed by a sinking pattern. You can also combine two entirely different sinking flies fished in tandem—a leech chased by a minnow, for example. It's a deadly tactic with lots of possible combinations, and you'll occasionally catch two bass at the same time. Talk about a wild ride!

My favorite way to rig tandem flies is to knot the first fly or bug to

ACCURATE FLYCASTING allows anglers to present flies to bass holding in small isolated patches of thick cover.

the end of the leader, then tie a second length of monofilament in the eye of the same fly. This trailing tippet can vary in length, but I rarely need more than 15 to 20 inches. The second fly—usually a sinking pattern—is then tied to the end of the trailing tippet. This method is less cumbersome and retains higher knot strength than the more common technique of tying the first fly on a 3- or 4-inch dropper off a leader knot.

Rig your flies so that the trailing pattern, on the end of the tippet, is slightly heavier or less wind-resistant than the forward fly.

Scent of a Fly

Many bass fishermen use special scents and attractants, but even the stickiest solutions don't adhere well to metal, hard-plastic or even soft-plastic lures. That's not true of most bugs and flies. Soak a deer-hair bug, fuzzy nymph or streamer in bass attractant, allowing it to soak into the material, and it will exude the enticing odor of food or pheromones for an extended time. It's another edge flyfishing can give you.

Good Enough to Eat

Sure, modern baitcasting and spinning lures offer superb imitations of many foods that bass like, but have you seen the array of modern flies lately? Many look real enough to straighten pig-tails at any grammar school show-and-tell, and a lot of these flyfishing patterns fill gaps that simply can't be duplicated in metal or plastic. Crayfish, minnows, crabs, nymphs, dragonflies, shrimp, frogs, leeches—you name it and some fly tier has come up with an amazingly lifelike imitation. Often, one of these bugs or flies will work better and

can be controlled with more finesse than a casting or spinning lure, but only if you have the correct delivery system.

Go to School

So a fly rod is no good on big, deep lakes, right? Actually, it's the nearly ideal tool for bass in open water. On large impoundments, when bass are chasing bait on the surface and when that bait is small threadfin shad or golden shiners—and that's often the case—a fly rod can deliver a more exact imitation than casting or spinning tackle.

True, long casts are often necessary, but a modern graphite fly rod can handle the task.

On big lakes near my home in North Carolina, bass boats gather in armadas to wait for schooling bass to chase bait on the surface. Most of these fish are small, but some schools hold bass averaging 3 pounds or more. Casting or spinning tackle doesn't always work because the bass are easily spooked or are reluctant to take large lures.

Last summer, I joined a handful of flyfishermen who were convinced that fly patterns such as thin balsa skipping bugs or Clouser Minnows dressed to imitate the threadfins would work. We stalked those schoolies in bass boats and smoked them while anglers with heavier tackle looked on in envious astonishment.

By now, you could be thinking that there may be room for a fly rod in your bass boat after all. The opportunities for school bass might be reason enough, yet remember that a fly rod is at its best in relatively shallow water where there are weed beds, lilies, emergent grasses, stumps, fallen treetops and similar cover. Farm ponds, small lakes and many rivers are prime spots, yet lots of large lakes also have smallwater characteristics. Certainly that's true of Okeechobee. Even big, deep reservoirs have sheltered coves, weedy flats and shorelines made to order for flyfishing.

Choosing Your Weapons

Today's fly rods, lines, reels, leaders, bugs and flies are generally superior to the gear available just a decade ago. For bass, an 8½- to 9½-foot graphite fly rod matched to an 8- or 9-weight fly line and reel will be your best bet, although some anglers find a 6- or 7-weight rod less tiring to cast and more than adequate when fishing smaller bugs and flies on calm days.

Many modern fly rods—especially some of the more expensive high-tech graphites—have fast, progressive actions that are designed for quick, long casts. These rods bend mostly toward the tip when casting and have stiff butts. Such rods work fantastically when distant casts and aerodynamic streamers, such as Clouser Minnows, are required, and the heavy backbones are great for hauling fish out of cover.

However, these stiff rods are not designed to cast big, wind-resistant deer-hair bugs, cork poppers or fluffy eel flies. You can improve a rod's ability to handle bulky bugs by overlining it—using 9- or 10-weight line on an 8-weight rod, for example. Though excellent, these rods aren't cheap. Expect to pay $250 or more.

If you're buying your first fly rod, to be used specifically for bass, you may consider purchasing one designed for the bugs you'll use often. For that task, you need a slow-action rod, one that flexes powerfully and evenly with an almost lazy stiffness over a much greater part of its length. Fly rods with these characteristics aren't as common as fast-action rods; however, some very serviceable graphite bass rods are available at prices ranging from $100 to $200.

When looking for a fly reel for bass, remember that you don't need a precision stainless model with bonefish-stopping drag. Bass get mad and shake their heads, but they don't take reel-burning runs. Most single-action reels (opposite page) will serve well. However, if you're like most anglers, your fishing isn't limited to one species. If northern pike, stripers, big trout, salmon or inshore saltwater species are in your future, consider a reel with a disc-type drag. Several inexpensive to moderately priced models are available that can handle big species that sprint. As your fondness of flyfishing grows, these sturdy reels leave room to grow into.

If you're a novice, a few casting lessons with a good instructor will soon have you catching bass you might not have caught otherwise. And should your casting and spinning buddies ask about that fly rod in your bass boat, just tell them it's for fun.

No need to give away all your secrets.

PARTS OF A REEL

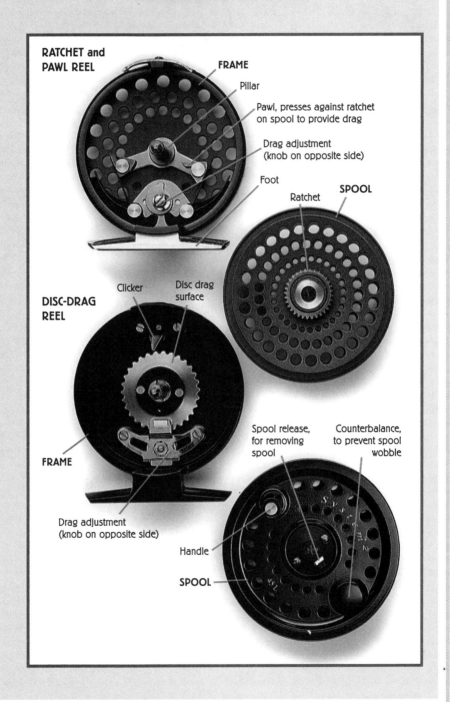

RATCHET and PAWL REEL

FRAME

Pillar

Pawl, presses against ratchet on spool to provide drag

Drag adjustment (knob on opposite side)

Foot

Ratchet

SPOOL

Clicker

Disc drag surface

DISC-DRAG REEL

FRAME

Drag adjustment (knob on opposite side)

Spool release, for removing spool

Counterbalance, to prevent spool wobble

Handle

SPOOL

Strategy Sessions

by Larry Larsen

Four bass experts explain how to fish weeds, wood, points and tributaries.

MIDSUMMER BASS FISHING CAN be a maddening exercise in futility. We know. We've been there ourselves, sweating in our boat cushions, muttering ruefully about the dog days cast after neglected cast. Heck, it's enough to make a guy go panfishing. But we don't like our fishing agenda banded to us any more than you do, so we decided to pick the brains of some boys who know a thing or two about turning on hot-weather bass.

They're professional bass fishermen, and what follows is tactical advice from these four experts on how to fish common structure types during the heat of the summer. We think you'll find their strategies a refreshing addition to your largemouth arsenal long after the other guys have roared home humbled by the heat.

Flooded Timber:

The spinnerbait search pattern

Ken Cook

"To tackle standing timber, I go on a
search pattern with a ½-ounce Classic model
Hart Throb spinnerbait, which has a single willow-leaf blade. I attach
a blue-and-chartreuse or red metalflake skirt and a white plastic
curl-tail trailer. I try to position the boat in open water, ideally on
some sort of an edge line, such as a boat lane, a channel ditch or a
fencerow, and make my searching casts at sharp angles into the
cover. Because fish tend to hold near the edges of such structure,
angled retrieves keep my lure in the high-strike zone longer than a
straightforward cast back into the trees. As the spinnerbait reaches
the timber edge, I slow the retrieve and continue working the lure
down the drop-off."

Other Strategies

BOB STONEWATER: "In flooded timber, I rig a live shiner under a bobber
so that I can track the bait. A free-lined shiner is more apt to get
wrapped up in the structure, plus that method of rigging reduces
successful hook sets. You can set the bobber at practically any depth—
2 or 3 feet in shallow water, up to 7 or 8 feet in deep water. I hook
the bait up through both lips—hook one through the dorsal fin area
or the tail, and it'll get hung up. In midsummer, bass feed along
timber fields that drop off into deeper water, so I concentrate near
the timber edges."

RANDY DEARMAN: "Like Ken, I use a spinnerbait to search standing timber, but I use the new Strike King model, which has what they call a "spin dance" blade shaped like something between a willow leaf and a Colorado blade. I stick with the ½-ounce size in chartreuse if the water is murky, and go with a white or white-chartreuse combination when it's clear. Fish the bait in 1 foot of water or 6 feet down—let the fish tell you how deep they want it—but once it drops to the desired depth, retrieve it as fast as you can."

Strategy #2

Emergent Vegetation:
The wild shiner float pattern

Bob Stonewater

"If the weed beds I'm fishing have stalks anchored to the bottom, I'll fish a shiner rigged on a straight-shank, weedless hook about 4 feet below a bobber. If the water is clear, I'll actually camouflage the bobber by painting it brown or dark green to blend in with the cover. Bigger bass are getting smarter each year, and an inconspicuous bobber seems to make them less wary. I use only healthy shiners and I'm careful to balance the tackle with the size of my bait—a 3/0 hook with a 6-inch shiner, for example, and a 6/0 hook with a 10-inch bait. The shiner is hooked behind the dorsal fin so that a gentle tug will entice it away from the boat, and it is pitched or flipped back into holes, cuts and points in the vegetation."

Other Strategies

PETER THLIVEROS: "Summer is a great time to use a small chartreuse or white buzzbait in vegetation. I use a ⅜- or ½-ounce Georgia Blade with matching color skirt and head. I cast to any irregularities in the cover and use a medium-fast retrieve—enough to keep the blade turning steadily. Fish the buzzbait right over the top of the cover and brace yourself for a strike."

KEN COOK: "In reeds and cattails, I flip and pitch a 7-inch, Junebug-colored Power Worm with a sinker. The sinker might be as heavy as 1 ounce or as light as ⅛ ounce depending on the density of the cover. To penetrate heavily matted vegetation, for example, I might go to a 1-ounce sinker, but in open reeds I'll use a sinker as light as ¼ or even ⅛ ounce. I peg the sinker to the line with fishing glue, which won't damage the line and dries instantly on contact with water. I work the bait into dark spots, pockets and points in the cover, moving along fairly fast trying to establish whether the fish are on the edge or back in the cover, which depends on weather conditions, sunlight, pH levels and other constantly changing factors."

Strategy #3

Lake Points

The bump-and-grind crankbait pattern

Peter Thliveros

"For lake points I normally select a ½-ounce Bill Norman crankbait in a shad or gray ghost pattern. The middepth bait runs about 10 to 12 feet deep. I toss it up right near shore and bring it back along the point with a steady retrieve until I hit bottom. Then I stop and let it float back toward the surface for 2 or 3 seconds, reel it back down until it hits bottom again and repeat. The retrieval pauses allow the lure to float up a couple of feet each time but keep it in the strike zone of fish hugging the bottom. Initially I cast the crankbait right up onto the shallows and bring it off parallel to the point. Then, I work my way around the point retrieving the bait perpendicular to and across its length."

Other Strategies

BOB STONEWATER: "On a lake point, I use a shiner on a free-line. The terminal tackle is simply a hook—a sinker limits the bait's movement too much, and I want the shiner to be able to move around down-wind or down-current from the boat to find where on that point bass are feeding. Once I locate fish, I might add a sinker or even go to the Carolina rig to better control the bait. If I'm fishing moving water, even if the wind is moving the water, I'll get many more strikes if I allow the bait to drift past the structure rather than trying to hold the bait in one spot. With your boat holding over the fish, cast your bait up-current from the fish and let it drift through the strike zone with the flow."

RANDY DEARMAN: "I agree with Peter that a point in the heat of the summer is a good place to throw a crankbait, but I want my crankbait to bounce off the bottom structure as much as possible, so I'll opt for a deep diver. My current favorite around points is a ½-ounce shad-colored Bomber 7A. Over the years I've found that points receiving an onshore wind are especially productive."

Strategy #4

Inflowing Tributaries:

The Carolina pork drag pattern

Randy Dearman

"I use a Carolina-rigged Pork-O in tributary situations. The Strike King model, which looks like a worm only it's made out of pork, has tremendous action in moving water. If the water's fairly clear, I use a white or white-chartreuse model, and if the water's off-color, I go with olive-green or black and blue. I position my boat over the pre-dominant point at the confluence, which is usually on the up-current side of the inflowing tributary. From there I cast inside the smaller

tributary parallel to its bank, and drag the bait along the bottom back to and up the point. The pattern is a sure-fire knockout."

Other Strategies

BOB STONEWATER: "I fish a live shiner the way I do a lure in the mouth of a tributary—parallel to the stream banks. Rigged with a small slip sinker, the bait is cast into the tributary mouth and allowed to drift back along the bottom. Though some people look at a shiner as something they're going to put in one area and let sit, I use that shiner like a lure, but I use it carefully—I don't cast it a lot. The mouth of a creek can feature edges, drop-offs and minor humps, and all have to be explored with a drift of the bait to adequately fish the mouth."

KEN COOK: "I go with a deep-diving crankbait around tributaries, especially if the cover is minimal. I use a 1/3-ounce, flat-body-type wiggling crankbait in a bleeding shad or Tennessee shad color. I target slack water areas like the edges of currents, eddies, pockets, and the downstream and upstream sides of obstructions like sandbars and rock piles. I position the boat downstream and throw upstream so that I'm bringing the lure back with the flow. Keep in mind that in moving water bass will generally hold looking into the current but not always right at the stream mouth. That's why you've got to work your way upstream, casting into the current so that holding bass will see your bait coming down toward them with the flow."

Secrets of the Bassmaster

by Joseph B. Healy

Four fishing patterns led Mark Davis to bass angling's mountaintop.

MARK DAVIS IS TIRED. HIS VOICE is raspy and his speech is strained, but not enough to disguise his honest Arkansas drawl, which is much more pronounced than another well-known Razorback. ("Hillary, doggonit, fetch me another one of them Micro Mallows, will ya honey?")

With a schedule of press conferences, ribbon-cuttings, and photo-ops worthy of a commander-in-chief, Davis has reason to be tired. But what a way to go: He is now one of the world's most popular—hell, one of the world's greatest—professional bass anglers. And he's everywhere—pitching tackle for his sponsors, slinging crankbaits on cable TV, smiling from the cover of any number of fishing magazines. If he wasn't so modest—an anomaly in a sport quick to pat itself on the back—maybe Davis would tell you about it. Instead he just drawls, "Well, sir, I paid muh dues."

And now his dues are paying him back. In 1995, Davis won both the B.A.S.S. Masters Classic championship and the B.A.S.S. Angler of the Year title, a grand-slam feat never before achieved in the history of the Bass Anglers Sportsman Society. The Classic victory alone landed him a tidy $50,000.

"But my good fortune didn't happen by chance," cautions Davis, who runs a guiding business on Lake Ouachita when he's not fishing or making personal appearances. "I spent more days on the water than ever before."

The secret to his success is a bit more personal than that. Until 1994, Davis weighed nearly 400 pounds. Plagued by constant fatigue and discomfort, he routinely swallowed painkillers by the handful to endure all-day outings on the water. Then, going into the '94-'95 season, Davis found the discipline to drop more than 150 pounds. His concentration and stamina improved and, not surprisingly, so did his fishing performance. In fact, the Classic victory was the first of Davis's career.

We buttonholed the man after a practice day on Texas' Lake Fork and, curious about the particulars of his success, asked him to name names: his favorite lures, rods, and techniques. He was tired, but not too tired to give away the four fishing patterns he used most during his championship season.

Shallows in the A.M.

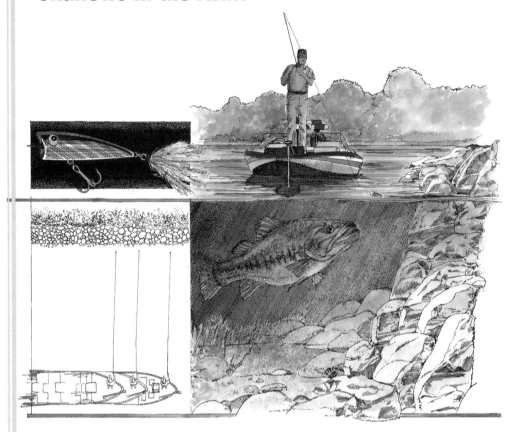

One of two patterns that took the Classic.

Off the Wall

Entering the B.A.S.S. Masters Classic on High Rock Lake in August, Mark Davis had a go-to pattern in mind: a chrome-and-black Rebel Pop-R fished tight along shoreline rock structure, such as riprap and sea walls.

"I figured this would be the pattern for the early-morning bite, before the sun began really beating down and the fish moved out of the shallows," Davis says. "And sure enough, before 10 a.m. that was the place to be each morning."

"I was running the banks, fishing the bait fast, in about 3 to 4 inches of water right up against a retainer wall," says Davis. To keep the bait in that shallow strike zone, he zipped along the wall, his electric motor set at a quick clip, while he picked up and cast often, bouncing the Pop-R off the structure.

"I wasn't retrieving the lure so much as moving the boat along the structure and making one quick cast after another, letting the lure just sit there and maybe chugging it once or twice. Fish literally pinned the bait against the wall."

On the first morning of the tournament, Davis drew nearly two-dozen strikes this way and boated four keeper bass, which accounted for most of his 13½-pound take that day and set the foundation for his later tournament triumph.

As an alternative, Davis recommends fishing the Pop-R over submerged grass. But there he uses a more conventional retrieve. "The key is to work it really fast," he says. "Cover a lot of water—keep it popping and chugging, almost walking on the surface."

THE GEAR

▲ **LURE:** Rebel Pop-R model P60, in chrome and black. Davis livens the bait's action by adding a white hackle-feather teaser (four or five feathers) to a No. 6 rear treble hook.

▲ **KNOT:** Palomar (Davis never uses a snap).

▲ **TACKLE:** Medium-action, pistol grip, 6-foot Falcon rod, with Shimano Curado baitcasting reel and 14-pound-test monofilament.

Deep Thinking

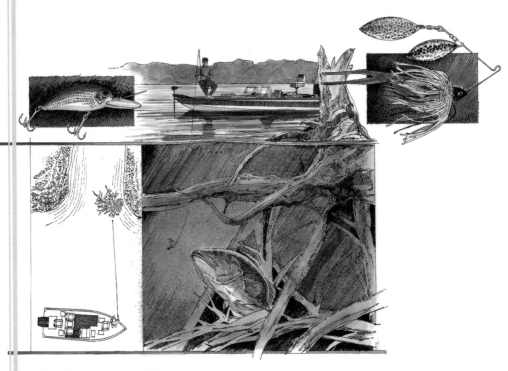

The change-up presentation.

Brush Busting

When the topwater bite fell off, Davis headed for man-made brush piles at the mouths of small tributaries feeding into the lake. "I had a few brush piles pinpointed with electronics (he uses a Lowrance X70A fish-finder) where I was able to hunt the fish one at a time," says Davis. "But long casts with a crankbait enabled me to find and fish additional cover once the tournament was on and it was critical to keep my lure in the water at all times. With a crank, you can 'feel' underwater structure.

"The fish were suspended 4, 5, or 6 feet off the bottom, in water 15 feet deep. Other anglers fished underneath the bass. That was important; I worked my way up from the bottom into the exact strike zone. Every bass I caught was suspended right off the brush."

Davis favors more forgiving fiberglass rods when he's fishing crankbaits. "The slow action of fiberglass rods won't pull the bait away from fish like graphite rods sometimes do," he says.

A Different Look

When that pattern petered out, Davis changed his tack. "I backed up and worked the brush more thoroughly with a spinnerbait," he says. "I threw a heavy bait to keep it deep; I didn't want it coming up out of the brush. When I felt my line in the brush, I'd burn the spinnerbait and then stop it right over the pile, which would get the fish excited. They hit as it dropped."

Davis combines silver and gold blades on his spinners. "You can't go wrong with silver and gold—they're my favorite colors when shad are the predominant prey species." he says. "Willow leaf blades also give off more flash and keep the bait down in deep water better than other blade designs."

THE GEAR

▲ **LURES:** Three-quarter-ounce Bomber Fat Free Shad in citrus; Strike King Pro Model spinnerbait with a blue skirt and pearl twin-tail trailer, and No. 4½ gold and No. 3½ silver willow leaf blades.

▲ **TACKLE:** (For crankbait) Falcon 7-foot Glass Crankbait fiberglass rod; (for spinner) heavy-action 6½-foot Falcon Low-Rider rod; (for both) Shimano Curado reel spooled with 20-pound-test monofilament.

Spin to Win

Searching unfamiliar waters.

Crank Lightly

Davis's initial comments sum up this pattern: "It's really pulled me out of a jam on several occasions."

Two such situations were tournaments on South Carolina's Lake Murray: The Megabucks in March of '95; and on Michigan's Lake St. Clair, the B.A.S.S. Master Top 100 a few months later. Davis finished in the money in both, and accumulated key points in his quest for the Angler of the Year title.

"It's a finesse pattern that works really well in clear or cold water in the 45 to 50°F range," he says. "I use a small crankbait on spinning tackle and light line. I like the spinning tackle because I can cast the bait farther than with baitcasting tackle. With long casts and light line I can get small crankbaits down an additional 3 or 4 feet. Basically the setup gives me more retrieval options.

"I target submerged grass, fishing over or along the edges of vegetation. I look for milfoil, hydrilla—whatever's there—and hit the grass bed with the bait and then let it float up. When you retrieve the bait, and then stop it, it's neutral buoyancy makes it sort of hang there. That's when bass hit it.

"Before and during the spawn, I target the inside (closest to shore) weed edges where bass are likely to make their beds," he says. "Then, after the spawn, I switch to outside edges, concentrating on points and any other irregularities in the cover's contour."

THE GEAR

▲ **LURE:** Bomber Deep Fat A or other small, diving crankbait.

▲ **TACKLE:** Falcon Big Mark's Cranker, medium-light 6½-foot spinning rod, with Shimano Stradic reel and 6- to 10-pound clear mono.

The Soft Touch

A twist for making plastic pay.

The Carolina Crawl

Any bass angler worth his Ranger knows about the Carolina rig. But Davis puts a spin on the popular method—a *slow* spin. "On windy days when I can't control a Texas rig or a grub, this heavy rig does the job for me. In fact, in the last 6 or 7 years the Carolina rig has caught more bass—and more big bass—than any other method. It's a finesse tactic that allows me to really feel what's on the bottom. And I use it everywhere I go."

Davis's favorite is a 6-inch plastic lizard. He uses a ¾- to ¼-ounce weight with a bead and swivel, and ties on a 4- to 5-foot leader of 14- to 17-pound-test monofilament, sometimes even going down to 10-pound. The shallower the water, the shorter he makes the leader, in order to force the bait closer to the bottom.

"More and more I find you need to fish the bait ultra-slow." he says. "Let it lay on the bottom sometimes. The biggest mistake anglers make is fishing too fast.

"I fish the inside grass line in the spring; when I feel the weight hit the grass, I stop it. In summer I go *into* the weeds and cast to outside edges, toward deeper water, sending the bait over the outside edge to the clean bottom, and bringing it back to the edge. In the fall I fish submerged creek channels, casting right to the lip of the channel edge where fish are holding."

Grubbing for Dollars

When lizards fail, Davis stays with plastics, but with a different twist. "I fish a curl-tail grub right on the bottom in 20 feet or so of water, targeting boulders and ledges. It's a great smallmouth presentation," he says. He uses a smoke or avocado grub on a ¼-ounce jighead. "Hardly a day goes by without catching a fish on this presentation; I can rely on grubs."

THE GEAR

▲ **LURES:** Carolina-rigged 6-inch plastic lizard, in pumpkinseed and watermelon green.

▲ **TACKLE:** Falcon 7-foot medium-heavy Carolina Lure Dragger baitcasting rod with Shimano Curado reel and 20-pound-test monofilament, with a 14- to 17-pound-test leader. Davis uses green fishing line, which he claims is less likely to spook fish during slow presentations.

The Rise (in Fall) of Bass

by Rich Zaleski

Here's how to capitalize on autumn's furious topwater action.

THERE IS A PERIOD ON THE CUSP between summer and fall when the morning and midday topwater action can exceed that of any spring or summer evening. Depending on the prevailing weather conditions and the latitude, it might last anywhere from a few days to as long as a month or more. But topwater bites are more about adrenaline than duration. And from a pure excitement perspective, the uptempo topwater action that occurs as summer's heat grudgingly concedes to autumn's moderation is tough to beat.

I was first exposed to this pattern by my Uncle Henry, back before we knew enough to call fishing tips "patterns." Henry was the closest thing to a fishing mentor I had as a kid. One of his first teachings was: "End of August, start of September, just keep heading up the river 'til you find bass biting on top."

Given all that's been "revealed" about bass behavior in the 40 years since Uncle Henry showed me how to catch bass on Connecticut's Lake Zoar with a surface plug, I could no doubt make this lesson sound a lot more complicated. But its essence is as simple as it is effective: About the time you sense summer's end approaching, bass will start biting on top in the upriver reaches of impoundments.

Henry caught most of his bass in those days on a white-bodied top-water plug with a red head. At least that was his favorite bait after he loaned me his only Walkie Talkie. Other than the fact that it had a wide, squared-off tail section and a vaguely "minnowy" paint job and that it was the only one Henry had—I don't recall much about that plug. I only saw the one he had, and only for a few casts before it disappeared into a commode-like swirl as I reeled it across the current. Perhaps the knot-tying skills of an 11-year-old were to blame for the loss of his favorite plug, but if Uncle Henry was upset at me, he never let on, and he even seemed to enjoy regaling relatives and fishing buddies with tales of the giant bass that popped my line "like sewing thread, I tell you, like sewing thread!"

I haven't seen a Walkie Talkie since. Today my tools of choice for the late-summer/early-fall bite are chugger-poppers like Storm's Rattlin' Chug Bug and cigar-shaped plugs like Bagley's Ratlin' Twitcher. In reservoirs with substantial weed growth in the upriver sections, a soft stickbait like a Slug-Go might get the nod. If the cover's really dense, there's always a weedless spoon or Lunker City's Salad Spoon, a soft-plastic variation of the traditional weedless spoon. One way or another, though, I'm going to see the fish hit, and it's going to hit a bait that I'm moving at a fairly good clip.

These upriver residents like the flash of reflective, baitfish-type finishes and seem to fall most readily for lures worked with an uninterrupted—if uneven—retrieve, as opposed to the gentle twitch-and-pause style of typical topwater fishing. The Pop-R and Rattlin' Chug Bug and their ilk are best worked quickly, spitting and jumping more than chugging or popping. Reel steadily to consume the slack created by the steady twitch you impart with the downward-pointed rod tip. Cigar-style plugs are worked in the familiar "walkin' the dog" motion, but at a tempo more reminiscent of an overeager retriever sloshing after the first downed duck of the season than a showy poodle out for a stroll on Main Street.

Both largemouths and smallmouths get involved in the upriver topwater action at this time of year, and both seem to respond to the same lures. If there's any difference in lure preference, it's that the smallies seem to be more frequently aroused by bigger plugs than largemouths.

The Weed Connection

Plug-size preference isn't the only bit of largemouth/smallmouth role reversal. Weed beds seem to take on added importance to smallies in this situation, too. Not that bronzebacks penetrate the dense vegetation very often, but they do prowl regularly along the outside edge of the thickest growths. Do they know that the baitfish harbored by the dense cover will soon be flushed into the open as water levels recede and vegetation begins to deteriorate with the onset of fall? I've never been willing to credit fish with a great deal of intelligence, much less prescience, but there must be something that draws those smallmouths to the edges of the vegetation in the weeks and days just before the weeds begin to thin out and expose the prey.

Meanwhile, largemouths in the same upriver areas seem more inclined to take up positions close to the bank, sometimes prowling inside weed edges but more often simply taking advantage of the current breaks found along riprap or behind stumps or laydowns. While the smallmouths prowl edges of the weed beds and flats in schools, largemouths seem more inclined to spread out along a stretch of bank or weed line and take up individual ambush positions.

Recognizing this difference in feeding behavior is important. When you're in smallmouth areas, keep moving until you get a hit, then stop and really work the vicinity. In largemouth territory, it's rarely productive to make more than one or two more casts to a current break after catching a fish. Saturate the general area with casts, but try to hit as many individual targets as possible, and don't work any one spot for an extended period. In all cases, keep your lure moving, because unlike the topwater biting bass of spring and midsummer nights, these fish are likely to lose interest quickly when the plug is allowed to come to rest.

The Soft Approach

by Rich Zaleski

What to do when spring bass give
your lures the cold shoulder.

IF FINDING THE FISHING TOUGH on your first trip or two of the season is disappointing, going fishless is downright embarrassing. How can such a thing happen in the *spring*? That's when largemouth bass are supposed to be shallow and cooperative.

Forget what you've seen on cable TV fishing shows. In the real world, largemouths aren't always "on" in the spring. Yes, they spend more time in the shallows. And yes, they can be very aggressive when they feed or when they're protecting their territory. But bass can also be surprisingly reluctant and temperamental.

Dial It Back

A tendency for bass to hold tight to cover typically goes hand in hand with a finicky attitude. In the spring, when vegetation is at or near its annual low, that "cover" comes in the form of timber, brush and rocks. These are exactly the situations that make most bass anglers reach for a flipping stick spooled with 20-pound line and rigged with a heavy jig. Instead, they should be grabbing a spinning rod with 4- to 8-pound-test and working a selection of small, subtle lures.

Think along the lines of thin-bodied, 4- to 5-inch, straight-tailed worms, 3-inch boot-tailed grubs, lightweight hair jigs and the smallest plastic crayfish-type stuff with very little built-in action. Select colors like smoke or green pumpkin, hues that blend in with the habitat rather than contrasting with it. Choose jigheads and slip sinkers in the 1/16- and 1/8-ounce range. The idea is, to sneak a bite-sized morsel into close proximity to a bass, instead of showing it off from several yards away and daring the fish to come and get it.

Fishing this way can be very nerve-racking. You've got to feel your way into the hollows and crevices where big fish are likely to hold. Once your little worm or jig is in position, use nudges and shivers rather than hops or sweeps to give it action.

You'll catch fish from the shallowest cover fishing with this slow-and-small technique, but it's been my experience that the best spots are logs, stumps and boulders that are just deep enough that I can barely make out a vague light or dark spot in relation to the surrounding bottom. Cast several times to these areas and try them from different angles, until you're satisfied that any fish hiding near them has had a look at your offering.

Remember: Always fish your lure as if you're trying to get it hung up. Because when the fish are shy, if your lure's not in jeopardy of getting stuck, it's not in jeopardy of getting eaten, either.

Bass Like Bonefish

by Jerry Gibbs

Sight-fishing—the ethical kind—for shallow-running smallmouths is a challenge with explosive rewards.

———————⌒———————

SIGHT-FISHING FOR SMALLMOUTH bass is a dirty word around Green, Sturgeon and Rowley bays and up at Washington Island in Wisconsin's Door County. "I wish people would just stay the hell away from it," spits state biologist Mike Toneys. What has Toneys so worked up is the "bed-fishing" that takes place when bass fishermen, unconcerned about harming smallmouth populations, dangle live bait in bass spawning nests. However, my definition of sight-fishing for smallmouths is another thing altogether.

Before and after the spawn, and throughout the summer, smallies in certain select locations around the country offer unbelievably challenging visual sport. This unique game has two forms: It can entail the stalking of feeding smallmouths in the shallows or it can involve casting to fish breaking over deeper water. Either way, you need fairly calm conditions for the approach to work, and fairly clear water, too. Zebra mussels have filtered many heartland lakes over the past few years, and that has meant far more clear waters, but I've had fine summer sight-fishing in zebra-free waters as well, scoring over reefs, along weed beds and shores littered with blowdown timber and off sandy or rocky spits. In all cases, the fish were spotted either below the surface or breaking before they were offered a lure.

If all this sounds tough, it's because it is. Traditional blind-casting to underwater structure will take more fish, no doubt about it. But that's not the point. Sight-fishing is a little like hunting with a longbow when everyone else is shouldering a scoped rifle—the drama unfolds *right there* within spooking distance.

In the northern Midwest, a couple of exceptional situations spotlight what this sport is all about.

Bass to Behold

In Lake Superior's Chequamegon Bay near Ashland, Wisconsin, just south of the Apostle Islands, Roger LaPenter sight-fishes smallmouths from, of all things, a Maverick flats boat. His best action occurs in 75° to 85°F water, but LaPenter starts fishing in mid-May in 50°F water, targeting staging, pre-spawn bass that are moving from deep water to depths between 2 and 8 feet. "We don't fish the nests," LaPenter says. "Matter of fact, I'm trying to get the state to 'post' bedding areas. We also try to discourage people from using natural bait—the fish are really easy to catch without it."

LaPenter's emphasis is on fly fishing. He targets submerged timber, old pilings, drop-offs and weed beds, including coontail, cabbage and wild-rice edges. On sandy flats he spots the bass as individuals or in groups of as many as 8 to 10. "They'll drop their heads and pick up a

fly just like tailing bonefish," he says. "And they *would* tail if it was a bit shallower." Chequamegon is a special place.

You've got to lead traveling bass with your casts, just as you would saltwater species on the flats. A fly or lure dropped on the nose of an incoming smallie normally sends the bass fleeing. In deeper water, casts to fish visible only by their surface swirls should be right on the money or, if multiple breaks are occurring, ahead of the direction of travel.

The smallies are primarily feeding on emerald shiners and spottail minnows, and that's key to the sight-fishing in Chequamegon. If the fish are feeding on crayfish or other bottom forage, they're difficult to target visually.

Current Affairs

In the Great Lakes and other big waters, current plays a surprisingly important role in sight-fishing. The smallies will nose into subtle flows and position behind current breaks for feeding and comfort,

MATCH THE HATCH

*B*ASS THAT MOVE ONTO SHALLOWS from deep water will eat what they can get, but they key in on prevalent forage. Stay tuned to your local progressive fish banquets. Dragonfly hatches mean you should use dragon nymphs; likewise with the big Hex hatches. Minnow imitations are almost always effective. In some areas, little green leeches—imitated with tiny plastic panfish worms or with Woolly Buggers—are potent. One more point: The shallower the water, the subtler your presentation should be. That means no heavily weighted spinners or flies. Ultralight plastics, balsa crankbaits and light spinners and spoons are the ticket. Flyfishers, meanwhile, should go with clear intermediate lines and light bead heads.

just as trout will. "I thought I was going crazy at first," says Bruce Richards of Scientific Anglers, who fished with LaPenter last summer. "Those currents change in minutes. You see grasses bending in one direction, then they'll suddenly reverse. The fish respond by repositioning, just like they do on changing tides in salt water. Then, you've got to contend with the wind. You think you have your drift set up for a current, and the breeze shifts and changes everything. It's very tricky . . . and fun."

I ran into the same phenomena last summer while wade-fishing the Beaver Island archipelago in northwestern Lake Michigan. A south-southwesterly wind would push warmer water into a bay with that exposure, while a colder north-northwesterly wind would have the opposite effect. I saw tide-like current shifts rippling the surface, making small waves where the water had been calm just moments before.

Guide Terry Van Arkel, who fishes the Beaver Island area, says that within a reasonable range the specific water temperature is not as important as temperature *change*, cold to warm or vice versa. In these cold northern waters the warming sun brings more fish onto the flats from deepwater sanctuaries, and Van Arkel's experience bears this out: His best sight-fishing is between 2:00 and 5:00 p.m. throughout the summer.

The water color is green-blue here, not unlike the Caribbean, and just as clear, too. "You can tell a bay holds colder water if it's clear green," says Van Arkel. "When it's not quite so crystalline—indicating the presence of plankton—it's warmer."

Bass moving in from deep water are dark and easy to see in the shallows. But like chameleons they soon lighten over gravel and sand bottoms, becoming tough to locate. There are clues that can help you spot them, though. With smallies, the tails and fins are usually the giveaway, and sometimes the side markings stand out.

Spotting the fish was one matter; getting a grab from these jittery creatures was another. To stalk these bass on foot, we would work the scalloped shorelines, motoring up to points or spits that divided one cove from another, then pulling in on the shoreside that would not be fished. The drill then was to creep commando-style through the sparse vegetation bristling upon the point and carefully scan for fish on the far side. Sometimes they'd be cruising a few yards out in the bay; at other times, they'd be only a few feet out, sunning themselves with their backs nearly exposed. You'd get only a couple of shots at them before they'd either take or dart off.

On other waters, including my home New England lakes, I've made good use of binoculars from a high vantage point on the boat, scanning weed bed edges, pockets in vegetation and near-shore cover. I've located both largemouth and smallmouth bass suspended inches below the surface that way—bass not visible without the glasses, fish that would swirl away if they were approached blindly. In these situations, long, accurate casts can trigger violent strikes. Try it yourself, the next time you're on the water. No doubt you'll find, as I have, that it's an addictive game, one in which the angler is hooked at least as often as his quarry.

Rats & Frogs

by Bob Gwizdz

They may not look realistic, but these weedless lures are the best choices for hauling largemouth bass out of thick weed cover.

UNLIKE THEIR TROUT-FISHING brethren, bass anglers rarely worry about "matching the hatch." Bass simply aren't that finicky. What kind of forage looks like a chartreuse-and-white-bladed spinnerbait with a red-and-black rubber skirt anyway? Yet we've all seen enough humiliated bass being kissed on Saturday morning TV shows to know how effective these psychedelic baits can be. The answer can only be that large-mouths are terminally hungry—usually ready and willing to eat anything that gets in their way.

LARGEMOUTH BASS LOVE REAL RATS AND FROGS, so fooling them with fakes is easy.

For the majority of fishing conditions, then, bass fishermen know they can pick out any of a dozen lures and pretty much count on positive results. But there is a glaring exception to this smorgasbord approach—when the bass are buried in the thick stuff.

When bass are loafing in the middle of an acre of lily pads, sleeping under a full carpet of algae or hiding in hydrilla, there is one family of baits that outshines the rest—weedless rats and frogs.

Rubber rodents (rats or mice) and amphibians (frogs or toads) are more than the other lures—buzzbaits and or weedless spoons—that anglers usually choose when fishing thick vegetation. Because they are true topwater baits (i.e., they float), rats and frogs can be slowed, paused or even allowed to sit for minutes at a time on those days when the fish take a little more coaxing. And coax fish they do: Bass will come from a long way off to nail a frog that's apparently hopping from lily pad to lily pad or swimming through the filmy algae on the lake's surface. I've even caught largemouths on baits that never got wet—I just rolled them over the surface covering of lily pads until the bass couldn't stand it any longer and burst through the vegetation to inhale the bait, lily pads and all.

Weedless, *truly* weedless, rodents and amphibians are available in several styles, but the best are those rats and frogs that feature double hooks with shanks that extend through the body and points that fit snugly up against the flanks of the body. They are the most snag-resistant and the easiest to use in the nastiest waters.

Because they have virtually no built-in action, these baits depend on the angler to make them alluring, and they can be fished in a wide variety of ways. You can fish a frog the same way granddad taught you to fish a Hula Popper—toss it out there, let it sit until all the ripples have died away, pop it once, then repeat the process until you've grown a foot-long beard. Or you can fish it just like a buzzbait, cranking it along nonstop until it slams into your rod tip. Generally, I prefer an approach between the two. Keeping my rod tip at about a 45-degree angle from the surface, I like to hop the bait along at a fairly steady clip with a quick twitching motion, reeling in slack between hops as I load the tip for the next twitch. But I've used many variations on each theme, and, at one time or another, all have worked. During a day's fishing, the bass will tell you how they want it.

Mann's Frog

Although a number of companies offer these baits, one manufacturer has even named itself after them: Snag Proof. These are the baits I learned to "frog fish" with (I prefer frogs, but this is a purely personal decision). Nowadays, several lure companies (including Snag Proof) offer frogs and rats that are pre-rigged with skirts and blades, the way I used to customize them. Mann's Bait Company offers a whole family of frogs and rats in a variety of configurations, and Southern Lure Company makes an attractive frog, as well.

The baits aren't ready to go right out of the package, however. Because frogs and mice come equipped with large, thick-diameter double hooks, the points are rarely as sharp as they need to be, so take a few minutes to run a file or hook hone across the points before you start fishing. And I also like to insert two beads or maybe a small glass rattler into the hollow body of the bait, just to give it a little noise as it scoots across the surface above the fish. But don't overdo it; if you cram too much stuff in there, the body won't collapse sufficiently when a fish hits it, leading to missed strikes.

Snag Proof
Frog

Always begin fishing a weed bed from the outside—the fish may be hanging on the edge or in open water just off the vegetation—and gradually work your way in. Cover the water, paying special attention to any changes in cover or structure. Creeks or ditches running through the weeds, downed logs, rocks or areas where two types of vegetation come together—say a patch of coontail in a lily pad field—deserve special attention. Don't let any surface weeds go unexplored; it's never too thick, nor too shallow.

There are two golden rules to fishing these baits: Don't give up on a cast, and never set the hook immediately on the strike. In my younger days, I'd scurry the bait from one clump of weeds to another—sort of the way a good bird dog works from objective to objective—only to find that the strike often came when I was lifting the bait out of the water. These days, I fish every inch of every retrieve, from the moment the lure splats down in the water until I've brought it all the way back to the boat. It is by no means uncommon to have a bass climb all over a lure 15 feet or more beyond the outside edge of a lily pad bed. Frogs are just as effective in open water—I have even used them successfully up against bare banks—as they are in the slop. So stay with them the whole way.

When you're fishing one of these baits, it's hard to miss the strike, which is usually explosive—often causing an eruption of water, weeds, bait, even fish, that rockets high into the air, followed by a reentry that sounds like a cinder block tossed off an overpass. And at that precise moment—when the angler looks out and sees a boil on the surface the size of a washtub—most beginning frog fishermen make their big mistake: They rear back and set the hook.

Only half the time, perhaps less, will an angler with a quick trigger finger connect with the fish while frog fishing. The rest of the time he'll wind up ducking as the plastic bait slingshots right back at him. Why? Because bass only manage to get the bait into their mouths half the time when they first strike.

That's why setting the hook on the strike is counterproductive. If the bass hasn't got the lure, you'll jerk it out of the strike zone before the fish has a chance to double back and try again. Proper hook-setting technique when fishing a frog or rat is to wait until you *know* the fish has the lure. Immediately after the fish engulfs the lure, lower your rod tip and crank up the slack, while looking for the bait.

If you don't see the bait on the surface, continue to reel—if a fish has hold of it, you'll feel it. At that point, set the hook, quickly and firmly, bringing the rod tip up over your head. You not only want to make sure you've penetrated the hard tissue in the roof of the bass's mouth, but you want to get the fish moving toward the surface immediately. If you give the bass a chance to ball up in the vegetation, you're giving him at least an even chance to get away. Set the hook and keep the pressure on. Get his butt to the top, and get him skiing toward you ASAP.

Because you have to manhandle bass, moving them quickly and forcefully from the subsurface thickets to the top, veteran frog fishermen insist on long rods with a lot of backbone and heavy, abrasion-resistant line. As you can imagine, your line takes a beating from all the junk in the water, so if you use anything less than 20-pound-test monofilament, you're being brave; less than 17-pound-test, you're being foolish. Heavy line will not affect the action of the baits we're talking about, and, when the fish are buried in the thick stuff, line visibility is hardly a concern.

If a fish should miss the lure on the first strike, the bait will generally pop back up to the surface. Let it sit for 10 or 15 seconds, giving the bass ample opportunity to come back and get it. If nothing happens, move the lure slightly or shake it a little bit to give the impression of a stunned, injured or dying animal. If still nothing happens, begin reeling it back in again with a stop-and-go retrieve.

Return strikes—especially those that come immediately after an explosive surface miss—are rarely as violent as the first. You still have to be sure the fish has the bait before you set the hook. I've seen times, especially in really heavy vegetation, when it takes a bass four or more strikes before he finally engulfs the bait well enough to allow a good hookset.

Building a Better Crankbait

by Jerry Gibbs

Berkley's new Frenzy series of crankbaits is the result of 8 years of laboratory testing.

———⌒———

I N MY TACKLE BOX, NESTLED alongside the year's bright new lures, are a few scarred old baits I treat like 18-karat gold. Bet you have them, too— plugs that due to some inscrutable alchemy have fish catching abilities far exceeding that of other lures of the very same make and model. What if you knew the subtle secrets of that appeal? One fishing tackle company thinks it does. Berkley, a

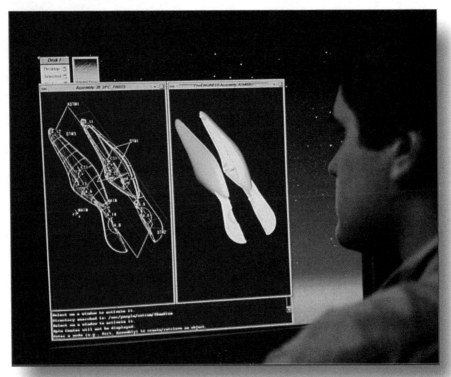

LURE-MAKING'S "WOOD WHITTLING" in the age of computer-aided design is done with a keyboard and mouse.

division of Pure Fishing (formerly, Outdoor Technologies Group), claims to have isolated the precise nature of that magic and infused its new line of crankbaits with it. Whether or not Frenzies can outfish other crankbaits will ultimately be decided by consumers, but the road to market for these new hardbody baits has seen some inventive twists and turns that bear relating.

Subtle Movements

Berkley launched the unique lure-building process by first surveying hundreds of recreational bass anglers around the country, asking them to name the bass baits they used most frequently under average temperature and water-clarity conditions. The four most popular answers, in no particular order, were the Bomber 7A, Rat-L-Trap, Norman Little N and Normark's Fat Rap.

Next, the company's scientists isolated the various lure actions to see if there were shared characteristics among the four lures that made them so effective. To do that, the basic components of lure motion had to be established. They include *yaw* (a lure's rotation around the vertical axis), *sway* (side-to-side motion), *surge* (front-to-back motion), *roll* (rotation around the horizontal axis), *heave* (up-and-down movement) and *pitch* (degree of displacement from the horizontal, or swimming, position).

Running each of the popular baits in Berkley's custom flow tank—a water tunnel similar to wind tunnels used by the aeronautics industry—the company's researchers were able to isolate these six components of lure motion with a computer-driven video camera.

The next piece of the puzzle was determining which of these precise motions make bass strike. The researchers built prototype lures of varying sizes that emphasized or eliminated specific movements and watched as a mobile robot pulled these lures—and the four popular crankbaits—around a tank of hatchery-reared bass that had never before seen a lure. Specifically, the scientists monitored the approaches, strikes and intensity of strikes that the various lures generated in the fish.

The Results

Eight years and some 20,000 fish later, it was determined that bass prefer neither exceedingly long, skinny shapes nor short, fat lures, but a shape somewhere in the middle. But that's not all—not by a long shot.

"Certain types of crankbaits attract fish well, but don't generate serious hits, says Berkley biologist Dr. Keith Jones. "Bass often approach the lipless Rat-L-Trap, for example, and sometimes bump the bait with a closed mouth, and in the course of investigating it they sometimes got hooked under the jaw. The Fat Rap, on the other hand, doesn't attract fish as well, but when bass see it there's a better strike reaction. What this might suggest is that Rat-L-Traps are great lures by virtue of the number of fish they attract, but if there are plenty of fish present or the bass can see the lure from a distance, perhaps the Fat Rap action is better."

Berkley Frenzy

The prototype lures that Jones and his team built went through hundreds of subtly different incarnations. Trimming the bills reduced oscillation and, consequently, strikes from fish. The pull point (where the eye is mounted) also proved critical:

too far forward and it killed action, too far back and the bait darted too erratically. "Bass look for erratic motion," says Jones, "but it's possible to have too much. The fish need to be able to predict where the bait will be on its next movement. On the other hand, uniform motion seems to translate to them as no motion at all."

Part of that might be due to the fact that bass have the visual lock-on tracking ability of an advanced auto-focus camera—essentially, they can see things twice as fast as we can. (It's a neurological thing; bass have lightning-fast transmissions between synapses. Technically speaking, they have a higher "critical flicker fusion frequency," which is the point at which a moving object becomes a blur.) What all this means is that the moving image we see in a video appears to a bass as a series of still images—a slide show.

So what are the critical movements that bass respond to in a crankbait? "We isolated three that are far more important than any others," says Jones. Of course, with the research investment Berkley has dumped into all of this, the company can hardly be blamed for not revealing what those are. "Call them X, Y and Z, " says Jones, coyly. "A lure that has these three movements is a better lure under average fishing conditions."

Professional Opinion

Watching Berkley's lipped Frenzies hovering in an observation tank, I did notice a subtle side-to-side darting action. It wasn't as pronounced as in, say, Storm's popular Hot'N Tot, which is so effective on walleyes, but it was definitely there. I would have loved to have compared slow-motion footage of the action with that of the other top baits. Alas, that too is classified. However, when I fished the baits I found that they give strong, consistent feedback, or "feel," through the rod. I was sure the lures were working, vibrating hard, and I was able to detect the slightest variance in action.

Lest you think this was entirely a laboratory-spawned tackle project, Berkley sought the input of top bass pros Gary Kline and Jay Yelas to ensure that their 8-year scientific investment translated into a lure anglers would use. Two things the pros wanted were "trackability" (a lure's ability to regain its trajectory after deflecting off underwater objects) and a steep dive curve (a bait that quickly digs down to maximum depth and stays there longer). In both regards, the Frenzies excel. Another neat feature is the internal weight-transfer

THE TESTING FACILITY at Pure Fishing allows scientists to view lures in a way that has never before been possible.

system, which moves a lead ball to the rear of the lure when it's cast, preventing "pinwheeling."

"Remember that these lures were designed for bass," says Keith Jones. "They'll take other fish, sure, but it's largemouth bass in the most common fishing conditions—what we call 'the zone'—for which we built them. Water temperature, clarity and current all affect a bass's willingness to attack, and the next series we make might be aimed at particular niche conditions."

Exactly what those niche-condition lures might be, Jones would only hint at. "From our tests I can't say rattling sound is that important to bass, but scent is. In one experiment with a Shad Rap, we trimmed out the back, fitted in a sponge and tested it with our PowerBait scent. One bass hit the lure *17 times*. So there's potential there, but if anglers do this kind of tweaking themselves they'll alter the lure's action. Besides, who would bother adding new scent every dozen casts or so?"

If a largemouth bass will hit a lure 17 times, John, the question just might be "who wouldn't?"

Hooked On Sonics

by Doug Hannon

Before you tie on that clicking, ticking, buzzing, whirring, rattling marching-band of a bass lure, consider a few surprising facts about what largemouths actually hear under water.

A BASS BOAT SETTLES DOWN TO A quiet drift over a shallow point extending into a vast basin of open water. The angler picks up a rod, unhooks a BB-filled minnow plug from the rod's first guide and launches a long downwind cast. Then he begins his familiar, steady retrieve, without a clue that—for better or worse—his rattling lure is broadcasting a din to every bass within a quarter-mile of the boat.

The characteristics of underwater sound are truly a believe-it-or-not story. Before man was a technological presence in the oceans of the world, it's believed that pods of gray whales, using their highly developed language of "songs," could audibly communicate with other schools at distances of up to 6,000 miles. What's more, these songs are not highly specialized sonar signals, but sound signals that fall well within the frequency range of the human voice. Today, however, due to the racket of large-scale shipping and other sources of submarine noise pollution, that hearing range has been cut to a couple hundred miles at best. It's no wonder that these communication dependent mammals frequently lose their bearings and become beached.

Extreme examples of animals using sound in an air environment—such as owls acoustically locating prey in darkness and bats using sonar to catch insects in flight—pale in comparison to what fish and aquatic mammals can hear. In studies, blindfolded porpoises have distinguished between two cylindrical rods that differ in size by only a hundredth of an inch by emitting clicking sounds and analyzing their echo.

So, how do whales, porpoises . . . and bass achieve such feats of aural excellence? Count out advanced ear development. In bass, that organ is simplicity defined. The fact is, the dynamics of underwater sound transmission are so impressive that most fish and aquatic mammals simply don't require the sophisticated ears that have evolved to capture airborne noises.

The Water Medium

For humans to hear it, sound must be collected with the outer ear and funneled through a small hole to resonate the eardrum, which then conveys the sound through a series of tiny bones to the inner ear. Animals that possess large external ears and ear openings, like foxes and deer, can hear much better than animals with relatively small ears, like people.

But that's in the terrestrial world. The body of a bass is about the same density as water. Sounds from every direction pass right through the fish, virtually unhindered, to its inner ear. Therefore, there's no need to collect sound with elaborate external appendages. Furthermore, sound travels at 1,087 feet per second through air; it travels at 4,818 feet per second through water. So efficient is the transmission of sound under water that the energy of an exploding firecracker can seriously injure or even kill a submerged man. (On an interesting side note, the ability of sound to travel from one medium to another is dictated by the difference in density between the two media. Water is 800 times denser than air, and allows only one ten-thousandth of the sound energy from above water to penetrate the surface. Which is why your partner's barking at you to "shut up, you're spooking the fish" is probably misplaced criticism.)

Dinner Bell or Death Knell?

So what do bass hear when a fisherman retrieves a noisemaking lure like a Rat-L-Trap through the water? It is certainly not a natural sound. If minnows made that kind of a ruckus there would be so much background noise under water no fish could make sense of the acoustic riot. Still, I believe there are times when such sound chambers in a lure are helpful, just as there are times when they are not.

My belief that even unnatural sounds can sometimes be helpful is based on several factors. Chief among them is the fact that a bass is a predator, and one of the fundamental predatory principles is optimism. Anything a predator senses in its environment is viewed first and foremost with the "hope" that it represents a feeding opportunity. However natural or unnatural a stimulus may seem, it is a bass' instinct to investigate and determine whether it amounts to a chance for a meal.

Most of the ways humans locate sounds are based on the fact that sound travels so inefficiently in air. Amplitude drops off sharply with distance, so we use clues like loudness and differences in volume between the left and right ear to locate the source of a sound. Conversely, sound travels with such incredible efficiency under water that a rattling lure produces almost the same volume at 200 yards as it does when it's only a few feet away. So the volume of a noise is of almost no help to a bass in locating its source. And because waterborne sound passes virtually resistance-free through a fish's body, the noise reaches both of the fish's ears at the same time without giving any impression of the sound's direction.

Water's efficiency as a conveyor of sound is a product of it being noncompressible (unlike air, it can't be squeezed; if it could, the weight of the liquid above it would collapse water at the bottom of the ocean into a solid mass), which is why sound moves through

water much as it would through a solid substance. Imagine workmen servicing a radiator pipe in an old building. Once the hammering starts, you might have to look around to assure yourself the banging is not being done in the room in which you are standing, even though the workers might be several floors and a considerable distance away. But, if that particular pipe is not connected to your radiator and you can even faintly hear the workmen through the walls, you'll have a fairly good idea of which direction the noise is coming from. Put another way, if you've ever heard the sound of a boat engine from under water, you know that to place the source of the sound you needed to lift your head above water to hear the sound in air.

Now, imagine the quiet underwater world of the bass being invaded by the loud sound of a rattling lure. The fish's senses are aroused, and curiosity brings it out to look for the source. Unaware that the lure is creating the sound, the bass spots the plug, ignores the buzzing and strikes. In this instance it could be said that an unnatural sound had a positive influence on the catching of the fish. Still, the influence was incidental.

Sweet Sounds

Sound, like any other aspect of a fishing lure, is a tool for anglers to use when the time is right. Neither I, nor anyone else, can tell you all the rules for determining the best time to use sound, but I can tell you that it is certainly not "all of the time," as purveyors of rattling lures would love to have you believe.

It is also important to define the type of noise a lure makes. Subtle, relatively quiet clickers, like those inserted into plastic worms, are less likely to be off-putting to fish than a hollow plastic plug filled with BBs or a slab of lead. I reserve the use of the loudest lures for deep water and open spaces, or for situations when the fish are extremely active and responding to things like bright colors and fast retrieves.

When I'm after savvy, more experienced fish, I try to keep my approach as true-to-life as possible, even though I'm aware that there are plenty of big fish caught on noisemaking plugs. Some of the most natural, albeit quiet, noises emitted by lures are those made when they bump rocks, trees and other underwater structure. Perhaps this is one reason for the long-standing success of lures that have always been categorized as "quiet," like soft plastics. Their action comes

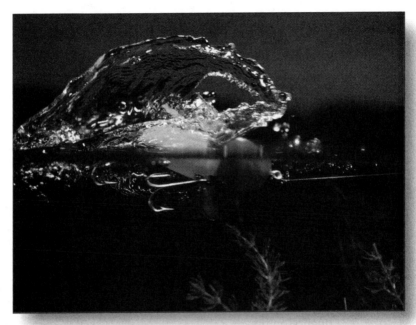

SURFACE LURES, like this crawler, make the sound of an easy bass meal.

from erratic retrieves and from contact with underwater objects—contact that creates subtle sounds bass are accustomed to hearing from their natural prey.

Other natural sounds you can use are the surface disturbances made by poppers, prop baits, chuggers and even buzzbaits. And if you're wondering where spinnerbaits—one of the oldest and most consistent producers of bass—fit into all of this, consider this little-known fact: Tests have proven that spinnerbaits are virtually soundless in the water, their blades turning in one direction in harmony with the flow of the water. The throb we feel during the retrieve, the one most of us think is caused by a violent underwater vibration, is simply the weight of the blade tugging on the line, like an out-of-balance tire shaking the steering wheel of a car.

Spinnerbaits are consistent with the rules of "quiet baits," in that they are much more effective when they're fished through, or bounced off of, underwater structure, creating their version of a natural sound. In that sense, bass fishing is a lot like deer hunting: The soft sound of a twig breaking behind you in the woods can be much more important than the loud roar of a jetliner overhead.

Smallmouths and Minnows

by Jerry Gibbs

Bait-fishing and catch-and-release are no longer mutually exclusive.

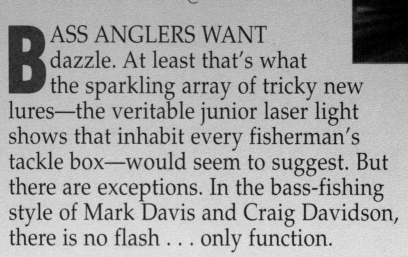

BASS ANGLERS WANT dazzle. At least that's what the sparkling array of tricky new lures—the veritable junior laser light shows that inhabit every fisherman's tackle box—would seem to suggest. But there are exceptions. In the bass-fishing style of Mark Davis and Craig Davidson, there is no flash . . . only function.

When Craig and Mark (no relation to Mark Davis the touring pro) were kids, buzzing Mepps spinners for smallmouths in the rich farmland creeks around Lebanon, Indiana, was the way everyone fished. But when high, cold water arrived each spring, the bass weren't inclined to chase down lures, even Mepps spinners. So Craig and Mark took the next logical step, which was to try the real thing. The

two began seining live minnows, and, not surprisingly, they caught bass when other anglers were getting blanked.

In the spring, live minnows would find big smallies for the two anglers in the mouths of tiny tributaries and irrigation outflows. Sometimes these tribs were only 2 feet wide, but their water was often warm enough to attract forage. Lively bait-fishing taught the young anglers something else: They had been walking where they should have been fishing. The springtime smallies, they found, would hang in slow current and slack water close to shore, especially in places where the main channel would veer close enough to form an easy retreat option for the fish. Even the smallest of cuts and irregularities along these shores deflected enough current to hold fish. And scallops in the banks, they found, generated eddies, frequently reversing the current so that bass would face *downriver*.

The downstream sides of gravel points and bars are also great places to swim minnows, as are the down-current sides of mid-river islands. Usually a lip and a drop-off are present where the river rejoins below an island. Fish the rocks and gravel above and over that lip, and also the troubled, swirling water just downstream. Sand/gravel flats on inside bends are also worth a try—anything with an irregular, rocky strata or sand/gravel mix.

Although a rocky, uneven bottom is great smallmouth habitat, it makes seining bait tricky. These days Mark and Craig use a 4-foot cast net. The mesh is ⅜-inch, so small minnows can escape while "golden suckers," the hardy bait of choice around Lebanon, are snared.

Rigging and Circle Hooks

Rigging minnows is pretty basic stuff, though dependant on the activity levels of the fish. When smallies are *not* aggressive, use only enough fixed shot to get the minnow to the bottom, and attach no

BIG SMALLIES won't think twice about inhaling minnows up to 6 inches long.

more than a foot from the hook. This arrangement prevents the bait from swimming too far and allows you to fish precise targets. If you're working the water column from top to bottom, however, or exploring more extensive holding areas, attach the weight 18 inches from the hook or use a standard bent-up "walking" slip sinker.

Mark and Craig fix floats above their minnows when they're casting the bait to a far bank, running it down a current seam or along shore. That way, when the line begins to belly they can flip the rod high and actually mend the line to keep the float on track. You can't do that without a float, nor can you do it well with a short rod. I like a 7- to 7½-foot spinning rod for this type of fishing, one with a soft tip that won't tear off the minnow on the cast, but one with authority in the butt section. Long rods also keep more line off the water, cast light bait farther, and make a simple chore out of flipping bait just like you would a jig.

Fishing natural baits of any kind has always resulted in extremely high fish mortality. However, that's no longer an inevitable truth given the recent introduction of freshwater-size circle hooks. Ironically, circle hooks have been the weapons of longline commercial fishermen who have helped deplete many fish stocks. Now the unique design is poised to become one of the strongest tools for conservation.

But don't just take my word for it. Larry Dahlberg, host of *The Hunt for Big Fish* on ESPN Outdoors, has this to say about the new hooks: "In catching approximately three dozen smallmouths on each of three outings, I've had 100 percent lip-hooked bass. I let them eat a night crawler right down into their bellies, give them line, let them stop and park. When I reel up, every fish is lip-hooked."

The key to using circle hooks is ignoring the instinct to strike quickly, says OL Contributing Editor and largemouth bass expert Doug Hannon. "Just tighten up the line," says the Bass Professor. "The hook will begin to pull out and, when the eye clears the mouth, the hook gap catches the corner or lip, the hook rotates and the mouth is forced between the point and bend—slowly and deliberately."

"Circle hooks are one of the most important breakthroughs—in terms of conservation—in my lifetime," says Dahlberg. "Wouldn't it be great if they were mandated right now in fisheries that are being hammered by poor bait-fishing practices?"

Shedding Light On Nighttime Bass

by John E. Phillips

A strange twist of fate forced Pat Cullin to learn how to fish at night. What he discovered is nothing short of amazing.

———————⌒———————

THE QUEST TO CATCH A BIG BASS often becomes a long and solitary journey. The time, place and circumstances for an encounter with a large bass are often infrequent. If the monster does hit, there is only a 50/50 chance an angler will set a good hook into it. And once the sportsman starts battling the fish, there is a strong probability that the hawg will escape before it reaches the boat.

In other words, trophy bass hunting has three requirements: lots of dedication, two hands full of patience and a backpack full of perserverance.

Trophy bass angler Pat Cullin of Valdosta, Georgia, has coupled these qualities with his own bass fishing techniques to catch 101 bass—each one weighing more than 10 pounds—in a 2-year period.

"Although I've bass fished all my life, I've only been seriously trying to take a big bass for the past 3 years," says Cullin. "On the average, I take two fish a week from mid-May to November that weigh 10 pounds or more. I usually catch 150 to 200 bass weighing more than 5 pounds during a 6-month season. I fish five nights a week. "

Cullin decided that night angling would provide the greatest opportunity for catching trophy bass in his area, after reading an article about L.J. Brasher, a night fisherman who angles for big bass around Madison, Florida.

During one 2-week period in 1980, Cullin caught 25 bass weighing more than 10 pounds each in Brasher's "Lunker Zone—a series of lakes bordered on the north by Valdosta, Georgia; on the east by

Jacksonville, Florida; on the south by Lake City, Florida; and on the west by Quincy, Florida.

"I've discovered that bass in different lakes go on a 2-week night-feeding spree at various times. One lake may begin in mid-May while a lake 2 miles away may not turn on until mid-June. It might have something to do with the exact water temperature that big bass need to start actively feeding. But if you fish at night during the time a lake turns on, you are bound to take some big ones."

After extensive reading and intensive fishing, Cullin knew that the evening hours were the best hours to boat a big bass. But a strange twist of fate made Cullin's desire to learn to night fish for big bass more urgent—even desperate.

"Nothing ever gave me more satisfaction or pleasure than bass fishing did. When the doctors told me one day that I would soon be blind, I refused to give up my angling along with my vision.

"I reevaluated my life that night and began preparing for the inevitable. I picked up my fishing rod and went into my room, shut the door, turned out the lights, put a bucket by the wall and paced off the steps to the other side of the room.

"Right then and there I resolved that I was not going to quit bass fishing, no matter what the future might be. So with a practice plug tied to the end of my line I cast for the bucket in total darkness. Soon I was regularly hearing the practice plug hit the bottom of that bucket."

The days passed, and once his vision began waning, Pat prepared himself for a world of darkness.

"Because I would soon be blind, I thought that fishing at night would help to prepare me. So I went to local lakes I had fished before during the day, lakes that my wife could drive me to. I burned the details of the water in my mind: where the lily pads were, where the points came out, exactly where the boat ramp was and all pertinent landmarks. "

Returning to the lake at night, Cullin would put on a blindfold—so not even the light from the moon would aid him—run his trolling motor to what he thought was the edge of the lily pads and then move 20 to 30 yards out. By casting and retrieving, he soon learned to distinguish the difference in sound between the bait hitting the pads and the bait hitting open water.

Cullin also developed new knowledge of bass through a keener sense of hearing. "I discovered that the part of the lake with the most crickets, frogs and animal noises also seems to contain the most big bass. Now I don't know whether this is true because I concentrated most of my fishing time in these areas, but I believe big bass are actually more plentiful in these spots.

"Another observation I made was that the region containing the biggest bullfrogs tends to have the largest bass. I noticed that whenever I heard a big bullfrog croaking at the edge of the lily pads, it wouldn't be long before I heard what sounded like a belly flop under the lilies. The croaking would stop simultaneously. I firmly believe that big bass either eat or kill large frogs that invade their territory.

From this research, Cullin formulated a theory about big bass territory. "I think the bass is territorially minded. He lays back in his kingdom and watches over all that goes on there. When an intruder comes in and attempts to take over his territory, the bass charges out to attack. Maybe the bass doesn't mean to eat the intruder; just kill it or drive it out of his domain. "

One observation that helped Cullin arrive at this conclusion is that 25 percent of the big bass he catches are not hooked in the mouth but in the head, the side or the belly.

"Because a fish is not actually putting its mouth on the bait but instead using its body's power to kill the lure, it's logical to assume that the fish are not feeding but are trying to get rid of an irritation. "

On a recent fishing trip with Cullin, I watched as a largemouth attacked Cullin's big Jitterbug three consecutive times before the bass finally hooked himself. The first three times the fish hit, he would not bite the bait. Finally, on the fourth try, the bass took the bait in his mouth.

Cullin says he tries to "irritate a fish into hitting by fishing every inch of a 180° halfcircle starting at the rear of my boat and ending at the front of my boat. If there is a bass in my coverage area, my bait should be within striking distance at least half the time I'm fishing in his region."

The first night I went fishing with Cullin, the frogs were croaking and the crickets were chirping—but the fish were not hitting. From 10 p.m. until 2 a.m., we had caught only two small bass. Just when I began doubting Cullin's finds, I heard an explosion somewhere near the end of my line. A crater appeared in the water and a monstrous head engulfed the big surface popper bait I had been wearily casting all night long.

"Set the hook," Cullin yelled.

I reared back hard until the Shakespeare muskie rod bent almost in half. The bass's slashing head came up again.

"Set the hook," Cullin repeated.

"I've already set the hook," I said, struggling with the bass. "Why should I set it again?"

I soon found out. In a matter of seconds the line went limp and the big lure floated to the surface. Estimating the weight of a fish in the water is hard, but I knew that the bass I had just lost was one of the largest I had ever hooked. But now he was gone and I could not understand why. With five treble hooks on the lure and the hard-driving stroke I had used to implant them in the fish's jaw, there was no way I could have lost him. But I had.

"With these lunker largemouths," said Cullin, "you have to set the hook three or four times to make sure you have as many hooks as possible deeply imbedded into the fish. If you only have one or two hooks holding him, he may sling them when jumping or tear them out when lunging. But if you keep setting the hook until the bass is in the boat, you'll lose far less fish than you would by setting the hooks only once. It took a long time and many lost bass for me to learn that."

Cullin basically uses only four different baits. "The lures I find most productive are the Lunker Lure, because it can be cast into the pads and worked through them; the Hula Popper, because it makes a big, loud racket that bass can't seem to stand; the muskie Jitterbug, because it can be walked, waddled, plunked and continuously retrieved; and a modified Jitterbug that I designed myself."

Musky Jitterbug

Cullin's modified Jitterbug is an 8-inch-long x 1-inch-wide piece of cypress wood, with an aircraft aluminum lip. It has three No. 4/0 hooks (two in front of the bait in case the bass hits the lip and one in the tail so that the tail hook will make a sweeping motion to catch the bass when the bait is jerked), and two No. 3/0 hooks (placed right behind the front No. 4/0 hooks).

Cullin also paints the lip of his bait black so it won't reflect off the moon. I believe the bait appears more natural without the silver reflection—it may even spook the fish if the moon is just right."

Prior to fishing his homemade lures, Cullin tests each one in his swimming pool—not only for its performance on the water but particularly for the sound it emits.

"The sound of the lure is the key to making large bass interested. If the bait doesn't make just the right, *blub, blub* noise, I won't have confidence in it and won't catch as many fish on it. I continue bending the lip on my lure until it makes the correct sound.

"The first night I used my homemade bait I missed four big fish. The second night I landed a 10-pound and a 13-pound bass. I also had on a larger fish that snatched the rod and reel right out of my hand without slowing up. That fish had to weigh close to 20 pounds."

The only problem with fishing Cullin's bait is the toll that the 2¾-ounce lure takes on the shoulder and arm muscles of an angler not accustomed to that large a bait for more than 2 hours. You'll need plenty of practice with such a heavy lure before fishing it all night.

Cullin works all of his lures with a stop-start retrieve. "When the lure hits the water, I allow it to settle for a moment, because often a big bass will attack the lure as soon as it lands. If nothing happens, I give the lure three or four *blub, blubs* and then stop the retrieve. Then I give it another, 'stop and go.'

"I believe that the bass thinks the bait is in no hurry to get out of the area, and may in fact be thinking about claiming it for his territory. Now a hawg bass may allow the intruder to walk through his property once. He may tolerate it a second time. But after three times, that fish has to do something to the bait—either kill it or eat it."

Noticing the thick lily pads and dense coontail moss in the lakes we fished, I asked Cullin how he retrieved his bass when they dove into heavy cover.

"Most of the time I can work the bass out of the weeds. But if a really big bass gets tangled up, I'll jump in the water to catch it."

Disregarding alligators, water moccasins or any other danger that may be lurking beneath the lily pads, Cullin springs from his boat into the water and follows his line with his hands through the weeds until he can reach the bass and pull it from the cover.

"A lunker largemouth means an awful lot to me. One of these days I hope to catch the Florida state-record bass, if not the world-record bass. So if I think that fish is on the end of my line, you can bet I'll jump in and wade over to where it is.

"Another one of the reasons I can consistently catch big bass is because I always release all the fish I catch, except on rare occasions. A bass I mount has to mean more to me than just having obtained a weight of 10 pounds. A fish that goes on my wall has to be special. So I know the fish are in those ponds."

Of all the bass weighing more than 10 pounds that Cullin has caught in his 2-year fishing spree, 26 bass were taken from public waters and 41 from water open only to military personnel or retired military personnel. Thirty-three of the lunkers were caught in private ponds.

With various places to fish, tactics developed to catch lunker bass and innumerable hours spent on the water learning the structure, Cullin felt he could cope with his eventual blindness. But through the grace of God and with breakthroughs in eye surgery, a remarkable new operation has given Cullin 20/30 vision in his left eye with the aid of glasses, although the loss of sight in his right eye is complete.

Cullin used his visual disability as an advantage to help him learn and devise new methods of taking big bass. Now he is convinced that his night-bassing techniques are the best methods of angling for lunker largemouths. He plans to continue to fish during the dark hours.

Many outdoorsmen would have given up in defeat at the possibility of losing their sport, but not Cullin. Resourcefulness and the determination to continue fishing against all odds have helped Pat Cullin to unlock some of the many mysteries of taking big bass at night.

Something to Flip Over

by Larry Larsen

Done correctly, flipping is the best way to get at bass that other anglers can't reach.

T HE WIND PUSHED A SLIGHT CHOP across the lake's surface as I pulled into a protected spot against the perimeter bulrushes. The bass were in them. Movement of the vegetation and an occasional swirl told me that.

My jig-and-worm combination pierced the dense cover beside the boat. I let the lure sink between the rushes to the bottom. Then a lift of 6 to 12 inches and I let it fall to the bottom again. The slow jigging action continued about eight times before I moved the lure to another hole in the stand of bulrushes.

The boat was positioned right up next to the cover that I was working with my long rod. My first strike came shortly after I arrived and, when I set the hook hard, the heavy bass and I separated. The parting of my 20-pound-test monofilament was a sad lesson. With only 7 feet of line between a powerful 7-foot rod and a big largemouth nearly buried in a jungle, I was doomed to a broken line.

I quickly switched casting reels, choosing one loaded with 25-pound mono, and continued probing that spot. Without moving the boat, I quickly caught three bass that varied in size from 2 to 6 pounds. I moved the boat a few yards and hauled a good largemouth from the weedy environment. Within an hour's time, I boated eight healthy bass from the dense cover.

It's like that when you find a concentration of fish embedded in heavy vegetation. Stringers can be heavy because of the easy pickings available in the weeds.

Use of a long rod and heavy line to gently drop weedless offerings into tiny openings in heavy cover is usually called "flipping." With an underhand swing cast, the angler can probe cover that's impossible to fish with conventional methods. He can maneuver his boat in the heavy cover and sneak to within a few feet of secluded bass. When a largemouth grabs the bait, the stout rod provides the leverage needed to hoist it out of the weeds before an entanglement occurs.

Flipping is hard work, but it can be extremely productive. Many anglers tire easily when jigging a heavy lure with a long rod. A willingness to exercise gets you away from other anglers who simply cast to the edge of the weeds. Bass usually flee that kind of pressure by moving farther back into the thick of things.

Bass in the heavy cover won't chase a bait any distance. They are not aggressive feeders moving over a flat with sparse cover. These bass make their homes in the thick aquatic undergrowth, and flipping is an effective way to get at them in that environment.

The flipping method has been around for years but was not popular until two California professional anglers won several national bass tournaments in the '70s by employing the technique. Dee Thomas and

Dave Gliebe, because of their success in cast-for-cash events, provided the incentive that led anglers throughout the country to try the "new" system. Now, many professional and novice fishermen flip when conditions call for it.

The denser the cover, the better. Lily pads, bulrushes, reeds, sawgrass, and so forth often form thick masses of seemingly impenetrable cover. Bass burrow under the thick growth to protect themselves from predators and to find food and ample shade.

They can easily ambush prey deep in the vegetation and they take frogs, freshwater shrimp, panfish, minnows, eels, crayfish, and many other items on the weedy menu. With the abundance of food in thick vegetation, many bass congregate there for most of their lives. Extremely cold water temperatures may be the only reason why some weed-bound bass abandon their comfortable lifestyle, at least for a while, to seek warmer deep water.

We can sneak up on these secluded bass haunts and coax fish to strike. The paddle, pushpole or, more commonly, electric motor with a weedless prop can be used to get at some of the biggest bass in the lake. The most difficult places to reach often yield the most fish because many anglers are just plain lazy and won't make the effort.

When bass set up home in the thick weeds, they lose some of their wariness. Sounds that would spook a deep-water concentration of fish have little effect on those that are weed-bound. The angler can get amazingly close to a fish buried in the dense cover. I have used my electric trolling motor to take my boat into reeds where I caught bass within 1 foot of where the propeller gnawed at a stalk after the motor was shut off. It is still to the angler's advantage, though, to keep unnatural sounds quiet.

Flipping consists of lowering a bait into holes in dense vegetation and jigging it. The method is very efficient for presenting the lure to weed-bound largemouths because very little time is required to put the lure into another pocket if the first one doesn't produce. The lure is seldom out of productive water.

The angler, standing near the trolling motor controls, jigs the lure up and down in an attempt to arouse the interest of a nearby bass. Ten feet of line or so is usually stripped off the reel to allow adequate coverage. If you're right-handed, control the line with your left hand and maneuver the rod with your right. Use your left hand to grasp the line between the reel and the first rod guide, and pull the lure to within 4 or 5 feet of the rod tip. Use your right hand to then move the rod tip and swing the bait toward the pocket within the vegetation. As the lure approaches its target, release additional line with your left hand, allowing the lure to fall into the hole.

Allow the lure to drop to the bottom. Then jig it several times and hang on to the rod. The reel drag should be tightened all the way. When you feel the telltale tap you have to be ready to haul the bass out.

When fishing in heavy cover, excess line tangles easily. This can be very frustrating. When you pull line in, let it fall inside the boat so that it is out of the way.

If you move from cattails in 4 feet of water to bulrushes in 7, a few feet of additional line will have to be stripped off the reel. If you want to put the lure in pockets farther away from the boat or closer to it, line must be let out or taken in, but always keep the line as short as possible.

The fish may sock the lure hard or stop it and just hold on. They may mouth the lure or run with it. When a bass takes, simply set the hook quickly and haul it up over the gunnel.

Most flipping enthusiasts use rods at least 7 feet long with plenty of backbone. Special "pitching" or flipping rods are designed for maximum leverage and power in rugged cover. Sturdy rods of shorter length will suffice, but they do have their disadvantages.

A stout butt with backbone and a fairly flexible tip with which to set the hook are needed in a good flipping rod. When the bass is close and green, his initial power surge will often snap rods that are not up to hauling out the fish. The bass will quickly bury itself in the dense jungle—never to be seen again—if its head cannot be powered upward immediately.

Any kind of reel can be used, but most flipping pros use the baitcasting variety. A positive drag and thumb control are advantages of that type. A line that won't twist during a power surge that pulls out against a tightened drag may be important to flippers who go after trophy bass.

The line should be a premium-quality, abrasion-resistant monofilament testing 20 to 30 pounds. It should be low-stretch and tough enough to survive the constant contact with heavy weeds.

The most popular lures are plastic worms rigged Texas-style, with a bullet sinker pegged so that it will not move along the line. A heavy hook that won't straighten easily is used, and the size may vary from

No. 3/0 to No. 5/0. Trophy bass in tight quarters can produce enormous power that will bend or break a lightweight hook. The slip sinker preferred by many flipping anglers weighs ½ ounce but, often, a lighter ⅜-ounce or a heavier ¾-ounce model may be required.

The sinker is pegged with a toothpick so that it won't "wander" away from the plastic wiggler. The special oil used to mask human scent and to attract fish is also helpful because it makes the worms slippery so that they move easily through the heavy cover. Without oiling, the worms cling to the cover. Loose sinkers also cause hangups.

The size of the worm varies, depending on the density of the cover. Shorter lengths maneuver better in the jungles than 9- or 11-inch versions. Many experts prefer a 'gator-tail type of worm that maximizes the action on a drop. The large, curled tail flutters as the bait descends. A meaty 7-inch model is ideal for most situations. Thin, curl-tail worms often wrap around the stalks of vegetation and tear when pulled free. Plastic worms that are too soft often allow the hook to penetrate the worm prematurely. Then the hook point hangs up. Medium softness, thicker-than-normal worms and ample applications of Fish Formula II or anise oil solve many problems in the weeds.

The color of the worm should be dark—black, grape, chocolate brown or purple. These colors are more easily seen by the bass in the subdued light that prevails in the weed jungles.

Movement is the key to success. The jig-and-eel works well. The jig-heads leading the pork or rubber trailer are usually equipped with a weedguard. Even the jig-and-grub rig accounts for some big bass. Jigging spoons have their place in the flipping man's tackle box, but they must be very weedless and they must be the kind that rise and fall in a fairly straight path.

A spinnerbait can be effective in flipping cover that is only of medium density. It should have only a single blade attached with a good ball-bearing swivel. A short-arm, drop-type spinnerbait with a weedless single hook is effective in heavy cover. The lure should be balanced to drop straight down into a pocket. A ⅜-ounce or heavier head spinnerbait is needed to work the cover in water that's deeper than 3 feet.

Flipping works best in extremely heavy cover, but shallow lakes with very little deep structure are also good. These lakes are generally weedy around the perimeter and barren in the deeper areas. Bass will locate in the weed cover of these lakes for almost all of the year. On deeper waters, the shoreline vegetation may harbor concentrations of bass primarily in the spring and fall and briefly during the summer.

Vegetation that is matted up or knocked over to form a dense jungle is ideal for flipping. If the area appears impenetrable, try the thickest cover first and then work sparser areas. When two or three types of vegetation coexist, try the denser variety first, then work the area where it meets less dense vegetation. Establish a pattern as quickly as possible.

The flipping technique is most successful in water colored by rain runoff. Bass are easier to approach in the murky surroundings. The entrances to tributaries are often excellent because of water color.

Fish the shady side of any cover that you come across. Bass try to avoid direct sunlight. They also move farther inside a weed mass during a strong wind. They don't like to be jostled by wave action.

Reeds or bulrushes are particularly productive. The taller and thicker they are, the better. Thick clumps often grow in fairly deep water hundreds of yards from shore. They are hardy and provide protection for fish. Weeds normally grow in sandy soil that is also ideal for bass. Clean bottoms are preferred to ones covered by silt and other dying nutrients.

A sudden drop in depth within a thicket often holds many fish. Fish boat-lane edges and other cuts in the vegetation. The action is always exciting and, when you haul a lunker through the surface on 10 feet of line, you'll know what I mean.

The Biggest Bass of All Time?

by Jim Matthews

A gigantic fish, caught in a tiny California lake by Paul Duclos, is a serious challenger to the mark of 22 lb. 4 oz., which has stood since 1932.

EVERYONE KNOWS THE BATH-room scale lies. When those of us who are overweight watch the dial spin to 10 or 15 pounds over what we'd like to see, we're sure it reads a tad heavy. Skinny people, nurses and doctors, on the other hand, wink and suggest the bathroom scale actually reads light. So whether or not you're in sympathy with what you're about to read may have something to do with the size of your gut.

On March 1, 1997, Paul Duclos of Santa Rosa, CA, was fishing 74-acre Spring Lake near his home. The owner of Ph.D. Carpet Cleaning and Restoration, Duclos is certainly no professional basser, but he's no weekend warrior, either: An avid big-fish angler, he was throwing a massive, 6^{7}/10-ounce Castaic Trout bass lure when he landed the biggest bass he'd ever seen.

"The first thing that went through my mind was, 'I've got to show my wife this fish.' It never crossed my mind to kill it," says Duclos. "I wasn't thinking about a world record. I was thinking that, before I let this fish go, I just want an idea of how big she is."

So he called The Outdoor Pro Shop in nearby Rohnert Park, and asked Ken Elie, the shop's owner, to bring a certified scale to the dock. Unfortunately, there was no one to watch the store, so Elie had to refuse.

Duclos then called his wife, Shelly, and asked her to come down to the lake and to bring their scale—the bathroom scale, with its big dial. There on the dock he weighed himself—180 pounds. Then he gently lifted the fish out of the water and weighed himself with the bass—204 pounds.

Even casual bass fishermen know that the world record is George Perry's 22 lb. 4 oz. bass caught in Lake Montgomery, Georgia, in 1932. If Duclos's fish was really 24 pounds, he didn't just break the record; he shattered it by almost 2 pounds. To break Perry's record, Duclos's fish only needed to weigh 22-6 (according to International Game Fish Association rules, a record must be broken by at least 2 ounces). Nevertheless, after a few photographs were taken, he quickly released the huge, egg-laden largemouth and watched her swim away.

Lest you think this is just another fish tale, consider that Duclos's entire story is corroborated by a complete stranger. Lou Skorupa, a Coast Guard commander from Petaluma, California, had met Duclos early in the morning on March 1 as both anglers launched their boats. Then Duclos pushed out in his 8-foot Swamp Scamper pram with its electric motor and began heaving the 9-inch Castaic Trout along the edges of the lake's weed beds.

"I thought he was throwing rocks in the water," says Skorupa. "It was pretty calm and I kept hearing these big splashes. You hear a splash like that, you think someone's catching a fish, but he was throwing this monster plug."

Duclos was fishing out in deeper water when the big bass hit, and the fish took the 9-inch lure so deeply that the lure was entirely in its mouth, one of the treble hooks pinning its jaws closed. With the fish's mouth held shut like that, Duclos fought it up quickly.

"When I saw her, I said to myself out loud, 'Holy Mary Mother of God.' Then I saw she was lip-locked and thought, 'I'm going to kill this fish if I can't unhook her quickly,' " he says.

Duclos propped his rod up and reached for the fish, but while he was lifting the bass, the rod and reel fell overboard. He slipped the fish back

PAUL DUCLOS moments before releasing his huge California largemouth.

in the water and hand-over-handed the line to get the 8½-foot Loomis rod and Shimano reel back into his boat. Then he corralled the fish again. "I have a live-bait well, but she wouldn't come close to fitting in there. I had an old stringer, and I put it through her bottom lip." As he headed for the launch ramp, towing the fish slowly along, Duclos waved Skorupa over and lifted the fish out of the water for his new acquaintance to see. Skorupa later witnessed the weighing and actually held the fish for one of the photos taken before it was released.

"I said to him, 'You *are* going to keep that fish, aren't you?' " Skorupa says. "He said, 'No, I got to let her go—she's full of eggs.' 'The world record is only 22 pounds,' I said. 'Yeah, Yeah, I know, but I'm gonna let her go.'

"I just wish I could have talked him into keeping it, but he felt good about letting it go, and I watched that fish swim away," says Skorupa.

When they heard about Duclos's big fish, bass fishermen and outdoor writers across the country immediately began drawing conclusions and leveling claims for or against Duclos, without checking the facts. One Internet site posted a photo of the fish and said the weight was 24.1 pounds and that it had a 39-inch girth (a fish that fat would weigh over 30 pounds). Some people suggested that the bass was actually a mounted fish. Of course, these individuals never contacted Duclos or Skorupa and never saw other photos that show the fish in different poses. Other small-minded bass fishermen leveled the usual accusations: The fish was caught illegally on live trout; it was snagged; its stomach was filled with lead or fish fillets; and on and on.

Duclos's wife was even harassed by some fishermen who belligerently questioned her about the legitimacy of the catch and why—if the bass was so big—it wasn't weighed on a certified scale. A handful of tackle-makers called Duclos to see if he would modify his story to say the fish was caught on their tackle.

"This is such a nutty industry. I'm happy I let the fish go. If I had kept it, my life would have been a living hell. Worse than it has been," says Duclos.

Many of southern California's big-fish specialists, however, called Duclos to offer support against the accusations. Ironically, several of these same anglers have all but quit fishing for big bass since their attention-getting catches. Bob Crupi, a taciturn Los Angeles policeman who received worldwide fame for catching and releasing a 22.01-pound largemouth bass at Castaic Lake in 1990, now spends more time at his other passion—big-game hunting. And even those anglers who still fish for big bass are frustrated with the politics of bass fishing. Duclos listened to their tales even as the same problems unfolded around him.

If the catch pointed out all that was wrong about bass fishing, it also showed Duclos the other side of the coin. One Internet site posted a phone number for Duclos—a previous number that now belonged to someone else—and the household received over 200 calls before disconnecting the line. When Duclos found out about the posting, he dialed the old number.

"I called to apologize for the mistake, and the woman told me that almost all of the calls had been positive, people calling to congratulate me for the catch, and for releasing the fish," says Duclos. "I have to say that most of the people I've talked with have been very nice."

Duclos and other Santa Rosa-area anglers feared that, once word got out about the big bass, their lake would be overrun with anglers trying to re-catch Duclos's fish. Spring Lake did attract a small crowd, but after seeing the small, weedy body of water, many anglers found yet another reason to be skeptical: They didn't believe the lake could produce or support a bass that size.

Biologists disagree. According to them, there are three requirements for producing a world record: 1) A newly filled lake with lots of nutrients; 2) Florida-strain bass planted as the lake fills (or after it is drained) so the first year-class of those super-gened fish faces almost no competition for forage; and 3) easy-to-catch winter chow (in the form of hatchery rainbow trout).

Spring Lake has all three requisites. It was drained in 1985, and a bulldozer scraped out the hydrilla. In 1986, it was filled again and 160 Florida-strain largemouth bass were planted. The lake is packed with small bluegills, and it is also planted heavily with catchable— read "bite-sized"—trout. As evidence for the claim that Spring Lake is capable of producing big bass, a 15-pounder was caught there just days after Duclos's fish was landed.

The largest bass, which usually are between 11 and 13 years old, are always from the first major year-class of Florida-strain fish spawned in a lake or some of the original transplants. These fish have virtually no competition for food and grow to astronomical proportions. As an example, Castaic Lake began its prime for huge bass in 1989 and 1990. Crupi caught a 21-pound largemouth to set the lake record in 1990. Crupi's 22.01-pound fish, Mike Arujo's 21.74-pounder and Leo Torres's 20.97-pound bass were all caught the next year.

Castaic was created in 1971, and the Florida-strain fish were put in the lake in the mid-1970s. Many anglers now believe the lake is past its prime. Occasionally fish to 18 pounds are caught, but none over the 20-pound mark have been reported since 1991.

Spring Lake, however, is the correct age for a monster bass. But if anglers there ever hope to see another fish like Duclos's bass, they will need to release large bass—those from 10 to 18 pounds.

Larry Bottroff, an expert on Florida-strain largemouths, likes to use the example of Lake Casitas, California, to show the power of catch-and-release. Casitas received so much pressure after Ray Easley caught his 21 lb. 3 oz. bass (the former state record) in 1980 that the odds of a big fish surviving long enough to reach world-record proportions were virtually zero. Few fishermen were releasing 10- and 12-pounders back then. But that has changed, as anglers like Duclos prove.

Duclos's catch was no accident. He spends a lot of time on the water, and he specializes in big bass. Duclos believes in stealth, and he fishes areas where big bass ambush the hatchery trout. His biggest bass before the 24-pounder weighed nearly 15 pounds, and he released it, as well.

"I never went in quest of the world record, but I always thought that someday I might break the Northern California record. People are saying things about me, but when you know you're good at something, you don't care."

The real question about Duclos's bass boils down to this: How accurate is that bathroom scale? The IGFA is the body that ultimately says "yea" or "nay" to world-record catches. Mike Leech, president of the IGFA, said he wouldn't speculate on how the record committee might react to the application, should Duclos submit one, except to say that "we've never certified a fish weighed on a bathroom scale. On a record of that importance, it will be examined very carefully. They will be very, very tough." Duclos took his bathroom scale to Total Scale Systems, which calibrated it and determined that it is accurate to the pound.

Does he have second thoughts about not getting the fish weighed on certified scales and measuring it as required on the IGFA record application?

"I wasn't looking for notoriety, or I would have killed the fish," says Duclos. "Whether it's a world record or not, I don't care. To kill the fish to have a world record, to have my name in a record book, that doesn't mean as much to me as becoming a poster child for catch-and-release. That's a reward because our fisheries will become better. That would mean more to me."

For the rest of the fishing world, it all comes back to that scale and how much you believe in it. Duclos believes.

"I'm not going to claim it's the world record, but, personally, I believe that it is," says Duclos. "I'm not a very religious person, but I was blessed by catching this thing. I got to hold her and so did my wife. Someday, when we're old and gray, we'll have a fish story to tell. No one else in the world has held a bass this big, except for me and my wife … and Lou."

Photo Credits

Photographers

Mark Davis
Mt. Ida, AR
© Mark Davis: p. 162

Paul Duclos, Jr.
Santa Rosa, CA
© Paul Duclos, Jr.: p. 219

Jerry Gibbs
Newport Center, VT
© Jerry Gibbs: pp. 180-181, 182

Bob McNally
Jacksonville, FL
© Bob McNally: pp. 140-141

Rich Zaleski
Stevenson, CT
© Rick Zaleski: p. 81 both

Illustrators

Al Agnew
Sainte Genevieve, MO
© Al Agnew: cover

Chris Armstrong
Jacksonville, FL
© Chris Armstrong: pp. 46-49 all, 61 both, 63 both, 67, 75 both, 87, 89, 133, 143 all, 157-161 all

John Dyess
Glendale, MO
© John Dyess: pp. 164-170 all

Steve Stankiewicz
New York, NY
© Steve Stankiewicz: pp. 134-138 all